THE COMPLETE IMPROVISER

Concepts, Techniques, and Exercises for

Long Form Improvisation

By Bill Arnett

On demand publishing by Bookbaby

Cover design by Bill Arnett

First Printing, 2016

ISBN 978-1-48358-899-5

Contents

1.

Overview

The first time I saw improv comedy was on the TV show *Whose Line Is It Anyway?* There would later be a US version hosted by Drew Carey, but the one I saw was an import from the UK. A rotating cast of comedy actors competed in fast-paced theater games that rewarded quick thinking. I wanted to try it mostly because I thought I'd be good at it. I joined an improv troupe when I went to college. That was 1992. In 1995 at an improv festival in Athens, Georgia, I learned that what I thought was improv was actually only half of improv. I hadn't spent two years improvising, I had spent two years improvising *short form*.

The other half of improv, called *long form*, asked its players to be patient rather than quick, to be deep rather than obvious. While I had a ton of fun improvising short form, long form seemed "cooler." The long form players were not only funny, they were also suave and hip. If I'd had an older brother, it's what he would have been doing. I moved to Chicago in 1998. Since then I've been taking classes, performing, coaching, teaching, and writing about long form improvisation. This book is a collection of the thoughts and techniques I've discovered. Think of it as a report to my friends about the cool things I found in my fictional brother's closet when he went off to college.

The first section of this book is a straightforward explanation of the many concepts and techniques needed to put on a successful long form show. I've also included some detailed exercises and notes on how to run them at the end. The next section includes sample forms and a generic structure that can be used to make your own shows. Along the way I'll explore certain concepts more deeply and, I hope, anticipate your questions and provide answers. I'll also talk about my training center, the Chicago Improv Studio, and how we put these methods into practice.

So What Is Long Form?

The "long" in long form improvisation refers to the fact that the players improvise for a long time between suggestions, often taking just one suggestion for a 25-minute improvised piece. This piece can be one long scene or a collection of scenes. Going without stopping for suggestions allows pieces to develop depth in both characters and plot. It also asks more of the players, who must now be directors and editors as well as actors and writers. The longer nature also affects the types of scenes the shows are made of. While short form shows have games that are introduced to the audience, a long form show tries to find its own games organically within slower, closer-to-life scenes. Typically, long form games are centered on human behavior (this guy talks too much) rather than on an external premise (each line must start with next letter of the alphabet).

Short form is short because the time between suggestions is short. A typical short form show (e.g.,

ComedySportz or Theatresports) will include an audience suggestion and a moment of audience interaction between every scene. This can be done by the players or by a host, referee, judge, coach, or director speaking directly to the audience.

Style vs. Technique

I don't wish to say long form is in any way nobler or better than short form. They're different. Some of the technique used to perform both may be the same or similar, but the differences between the two are stylistic.

There are many correct techniques for playing guitar. Style involves choosing specific techniques to achieve a particular sound. You could think of style as a subset of technique. The punk band guitarist will use barre chords, the country music player might use a slide or drop D tuning, and the heavy metal guitarist's legato technique allows for 100-mph solos.

Just as there is no universally correct technique for playing the guitar, there isn't for doing improv, either. A fast-paced short form show will require different rules to do well than a patient long form show will. At various points in this book, I'll advise you to say no, ask questions, and to not yes-and, depending on the context. I'll even challenge you to ignore your partner's choices. Doing these things won't cause poor scenes; it will create different scenes.

What kind of improv do you like? Fast, slow, silly, serious? Use whatever techniques are appropriate to make it happen.

In this book, all of my "do this, not that" advice will be geared toward creating a Chicago-style long form show.

Within the genres of short form and long form are sub-genres. If this book belongs to a sub-genre, it's Chicago-style long form. But no one took a clean sheet of paper, wrote "Chicago-style" at the top, and started filling the page. The "Chicago-style" tag was created by people looking at improv coming from different places and ascribing names to the styles that already existed namelessly.

If I had to define Chicago-style, I would define it as truthful improv that balances character and premise. No one set out to play that way; it's an after-the-fact label to describe what happens here. Words like truthful, character, and premise may feel like heavy concepts. I'll lighten them up with simple working definitions later.

A Brief History

Long form is a recent term used to describe a kind of free-form improvisation that's been experimented with and performed since the 1950s. The compulsion to perform an improvised play is very old and has gone by many names in the past.

Commedia dell'arte, which dates to 16th-century Italy, is one example. It relied on stock characters and generic situations that audiences could immediately identify with. The dialogue was improvised.

Modern long form breaks from that tradition by improvising everything, not just dialogue. The roots of this notion (or if not the roots, then the branch that would lead to Chicago) go back to San Francisco in the '60s, The Committee, and Del Close.

The Committee was a product of its decade: edgy, cool, and political. They performed written scenes and a structured improvised piece. Del Close, an actor and beatnik standup, was brought into direct.

4

He helped them develop a structure that began with asking an audience member for a question they wanted an answer to, like "How do you find love?" The group would improvise scenes and perform group rituals to explore the meaning of the suggestion.

A group ritual might take the form of a player repeating a word over and over again while the other players danced around him. Very organic, very '60s. The players also kept rehearsed character monologues in their back pockets, just in case things went south. (Today that would be considered cheating.) The show would end with the players stepping forward and answering the question using the thoughts and ideas explored and uncovered during the show, perhaps in the voices of characters they had played.

This loose structure would today be called a form. "Form" means a structure and rules. It was given the name "Harold" as a reference to George Harrison's response to what he called his haircut ("Arthur"). Del continued working on Harold in Chicago. It changed and grew. The scenes stayed, the rehearsed monologues were replaced with truthful monologues, and the group rituals became what are now called openings and games. For the last 30 years, with Del's spiritual leadership, Harold has changed and morphed and birthed hundreds of new forms and concepts that try to better answer the question: How do we improvise a cohesive whole?

Harold and its (his?) children are not the only answers to that question. Other answers have come from very different places under very different circumstances. There are many influential people in the history of improv, including Viola Spolin, Paul Sills, and certainly Keith Johnstone.

While the Committee form was great and entertaining, it had to change, because art isn't static. It changes and grows and asks its practitioners to do the same. There have been and will continue to be bad decisions and wrong turns in its life, but long form is a living art, and hopefully, in the long run, it will always be better than it was. The fact that it looks different every time isn't a liability but rather its strength. While some forms have been played and replayed for years, new forms and approaches are created every day.

What Is a Form?

The "form" in "long form" is an agreed-upon structure that the players use to create their show. This structure can be simple or complex. It can be defined by the order scenes are played, by the style the scenes will be played in, by a set of legal and illegal moves, or by some combination of the three.

An easy way to conceptualize form is to first think of a show with no form, sometimes called a montage. The actors take turns performing improvised scenes one after the next without any connections between them. Because it's a long form show, the actors will have to edit each other's scenes. (The often-used sweep edit involves an offstage player running across the stage in front of the current scene and starting a new one.) Perhaps all the scenes are inspired by the same source material, but their content and the order in which they're played are not based on previous scenes.

A simple form you could lay on top of a montage might be this: After the first three scenes, the first scene returns, followed by the second and third. Regardless of the content of the scenes or source material, the form tells the players what comes next. By having scenes return, you could explore the characters more fully by putting them in new situations and transforming the show from a collection of scenes to a piece that tells a cohesive story. The whole might now be more than its parts.

The job of the form is not to impress the audience with its cool twists and turns but to aid the players. Functionally, it helps the players to keep track of time, and it provides a structure for their thoughts. Artistically, it sets stylistic boundaries and opens opportunities for the players to build on themes, ideas, and characters already known to the audience.

A good form is the frame around the canvas. Its job is to hold and support the painting physically while complementing the artistic value of the painting with its color and design. Just as you could put a great frame around a lousy painting, a "cool" form may find itself filled with terrible improv. Ultimately people go to galleries and improv shows not to see the frames or forms but the paintings and the performances. A masterpiece without a frame leaning against a wall is still a masterpiece.

Five Assumptions

Before we get to the nuts and bolts of long form, I'd like to briefly discuss philosophy. I've been doing this for a long time, I've been surrounded by the best players, I've worked with some amazing teachers, and I've read some great books. I have also spent time scratching my head over confusing or contradictory instructions. I have struggled with the vague concepts and the ancient wisdom we are forbidden to question. This really hit me when I began teaching and would find my mouth saying things I had learned that my brain didn't always believe. Improv performance is an art, and while artistic concepts are imprecise and subjective, they don't have to be confusing.

My goal is not to discredit other teachers or overturn long-held beliefs. Instead, I want to start at the beginning, at our most basic assumptions about improvisation. I'm not so much interested in refuting the classic rules as I am in reframing the way we look at the process. If we can identify the common threads that run through all successful improvisation, many of our hangups and problems with improv theory simply cease to exist.

I could start by considering what a talented improviser thinks about onstage, or about what makes a good scene a good scene from a player's point of view. But I'd like to take a step back and instead consider what audiences think about as they watch a show. Not what we as players believe an audience thinks, but what a person with no knowledge of improvisation walking in and watching a show thinks.

Here are five assumptions about improv audiences. Throughout this book I will explore each assumption from a player's perspective and provide sound, actionable advice for strong improv play based on each assumption. It's from these assumptions that I draw my lessons and advice.

1. A truthful, reasonable, and clearly played scene will hold the audience's attention.

2. The audience would rather a scene or show start slow and end strong than start strong and end slow.

3. The more deeply the audience understands a scene, the more likely they are to be emotionally affected by it.

4. The audience will enjoy a funny idea, premise, or concept when it is revealed, but their enjoyment of the rest of the scene depends on how well it is played.

5. The audience does not know the rules of improv or your form and will not judge you by those rules.

The Chicago Improv Studio

While I was writing this book, some of my friends and editors told me that they liked it but that the concepts seemed advanced. They said that this book should be marketed to people who had improvised before. I was surprised to hear this because I had set out to write a book that starts at the very beginning.

In talking to them more, I realized that the perceived bias toward advanced students was rooted in the fact that I dismiss or don't use many concepts that those readers considered basic. "You have to start with the concept of yes-and," they said. "Since you don't, this must be advanced." I told them my reason for not starting with yes-and: players should play to satisfy the moment, not to satisfy an outside rule like yes-and. I told them of the wonderful successes my students and I had experienced playing moments rather than playing by the rules. It didn't matter. No yes-and? Then it *must* be advanced.

In 2014 I launched the Chicago Improv Studio to turn my theories into practice. Students are drilled on living in and playing the moment. The focus is not on successfully completing improv exercises but on having successful scenes, regardless of the exercise. When improvising onstage, a player must use all of her skills at the same time: scene work, ensemble play, concept of form, etc. Because of this, levels at CIS aren't broken down by skill. Instead, every level requires students to use all of their tools. As the levels progress, they must sharpen their tools to deal with increasingly complex forms.

I've been happy with the results so far. But the search for deeper truths continues. The deeper we dig, the more we learn. And to truly dig deep, we must be prepared to unburden ourselves of the biases and beliefs of the past. Rather than studying how people improvised yesterday, let's discover how we will improvise tomorrow.

A Challenge

The world is an amazing place and our lives are full of pain and laughter, tragedy and joy, terror and boredom. Improvisation recognizes the simple power of reality and allows all of life's richness to exist and be presented onstage. If something can happen in life, it can happen in an improv show. It won't just magically happen, though. We must invite it onto the stage.

2.

SCENES

The bulk of a long form show consists of scenes. You could get the brightest improv minds together to come up with an unbeatable form, but if the scenes aren't any good, the show won't be either. You could also put up a formless collection of skillfully-played scenes (a montage) and have a successful show. To be a good long form player, you must be a good scene player.

Scenes can be short or long. They can be started purposefully, with several well-crafted sentences that lay everything out, or they can start delicately, with a glance or a pantomimed activity. Or they can start truly spontaneously, as when a player accidentally knocks over a chair and her partner reacts to it.

Two Shows at Once
Scenes can be funny for many reasons. It's easy to see the witty dialogue and clever play, but because improv is created in front of an audience, the act of its creation is also entertaining.

Bob Ross, the frizzy-haired painter from *The Joy Of Painting*, enjoyed a long career on television, but it wasn't just his skill at painting that drew us to him. It was the fun of watching him paint. Similarly, the audience enjoys our improv but also enjoys watching us improvise. It's two shows in one. One show is our improv performance: well-played scenes, interesting moves, and fun callbacks. The other show involves the spectacle of people making things up in real time: the fun discoveries and occasional blunders.

Some groups like to have wild fun and favor spectacle over content. They jump on each other's backs, break onstage, and play larger-than-life characters. Too much of that and you look like a ham. Other groups eschew the spectacle in favor of content, playing their scenes with no affectation and avoiding fantastical situations. Too much of this and you might appear pretentious or – even worse – bore the audience.

Audiences may like a player with an exceptionally large personality or droll delivery even as his fellow players hate him for being selfish or emotionally unavailable. In this way, it's possible for a player to succeed and fail at the same time. A fun show is not always great improv.

Like it or not, you're in two shows every time you step onstage. You are responsible for both.

Different types of scenes require different techniques to make them successful. In fact, as a scene unfolds, the techniques we use to successfully play them may change under our feet. Some scenes might follow the lives of the characters, in which case it's the actors' job to portray those lives honestly. Other scenes might depend on a premise or funny situation that compels the actors to step outside of the characters and find humor in the circumstances. Improvisers tend to label these two types of scenes as relationship scenes and game scenes. In truth, every scene is a bit of both, and the flavor may change mid-scene. Game scenes are explored in their own section later. We'll start here with relationship scenes and strong scene play in general.

Here's a simple definition of a scene: two people being emotionally affected by each other's words and actions. Relationship scenes are generally played truthfully without excessive affectation. Having emotion doesn't require overwrought soap-opera acting. Usually a simple emotional choice is all that's needed to show that what's happening in that moment has meaning. Meaning doesn't require profound, galactic truths; it just requires a simple reason for the characters to continue interacting.

I went into a coffee shop and asked for a maple scone. I was told they didn't have any more. I pursed my lips and sighed. That moment had meaning. I was affected emotionally and gave an honest response, albeit a small one, to the unfortunate news that the maple scones were sold out.

Honesty does not require soul-baring, just feelings that are not contrived. Improvisers get into trouble when, rather than playing these simple moments with honesty, they try to come up with a witty response or a clever situation. They also get into trouble when they try to "win" the situation by refusing to allow their characters to ever be disappointed or wrong, things that happen to us in life all the time.

When you're onstage, you should be doing your best to honestly portray the life of the character you're playing. That character could be very close to yourself in temperament or it could be exceptionally absurd. It doesn't matter. Play the scene through the character's eyes. To quote the acting guru Sanford Meisner, "Acting is living truthfully in imaginary circumstances." I don't want this to sound heavy. Just like the words "emotion," "meaning," and "honesty," the word "truthfully" sometimes pushes us toward melodrama. But in improv, to play the truth of a moment is just to behave like a typical person (or your character) would actually behave if the situation you are playing happened in real life.

ASSUMPTION 1:

A truthful, reasonable, and clearly played scene will hold the audience's attention.

Since the invention of the printing press in 1450, 129 million different books have been printed. Most titles have been forgotten and have fallen out of print. There are, however, some famous books still in print and still being read. Some are really old. Books like *The Canterbury Tales*, *Don Quixote*, and the works of Shakespeare come to mind. They deal with complex questions of humanity and have so successfully captured the timeless spirit of humankind that they resonate with readers today.

There's another book to add to this list of really old, still-in-print books, a book I took as inspiration for the title of my book. It was written in 1653 by Izaak Walton. It isn't about kings or love affairs or epic adventures. It's about fishing. After 350 years, *The Compleat Angler*, is still in print.

Does it contain secret fishing knots and fly-tying techniques indispensable even to today's modern fisherman? Not really. The subtitle of the book is "A Contemplative Man's Recreation" and much of the book is spent in contemplation of what it means to be a fisherman. It spends just as much time on the psychology of fish as it does on the psychology of people. By his own admission, Mr. Walton was only an average fisherman, but for him the bait, lures, and different ways of casting were secondary to the spirit – the truth – of the fisherman.

It is this foray into the truth of the moment, and not just into fishing technique, that has held our attention and kept *The Compleat Angler* in print.

What can we say about our improv scenes? Are they just a demonstration of proper technique, or do they feature real humans living real human lives? The first assumption – a truthful, reasonable, and clearly played scene will hold an audience's attention – illustrates a perfect baseline for our improv scenes. We don't need to be funny to capture and hold the audience's attention. We just need to be real.

Being real onstage, something called drama, has worked successfully for countless not-funny books, plays, and movies. So why can't it work for improv? For one thing, players often hear "drama" and "play real" and do scenes about people with cancer, but drama and reality simply mean portraying the people and behaviors of typical daily life, not just the occasional heightened experiences or brief moments of tragedy.

Attempting to play true to life can be tricky for experienced improvisers because it puts us in conflict with some traditional improv rules. Much of the well-meaning improv advice that I was trained with (don't say no, don't ask questions, don't talk about people that aren't there) prevents many of the real moments that happen to us in our lives from ever appearing onstage. In my life, I have said no, asked questions, and talked about people that weren't there. So, based on my first assumption, out go the old rules and in comes this advice:

Playing the simple reality that your scene presents to you is always a strong and correct choice.

Simple Scenes

If the first assumption is true, then the easiest scenes to play should be those in which we portray people close to ourselves, in situations from our own lives. Since it's a world we know very well, little has to be invented. A scene could be about about two deli employees prepping for the lunch rush or two office workers making weekend plans in the break room. The characters live in the same world we do, one that is very familiar to us, making them easier to understand.

It is also a world familiar to the audience, and that's what makes simple scenes powerful. The audience begins with a understanding of the moments and characters. They can see, understand, and (most importantly) empathize with the characters and what is happening to them.

Another conclusion from the first assumption is this: in pursuit of being truthful, anything you do in life you have permission to do onstage. You may cry, laugh, lie well, lie poorly, say no, ask questions, ignore, talk about people who aren't there, get frustrated, annoy, be annoyed, be a scumbag, be saccharine-sweet, talk about the past, talk about the future, be old friends, be old friends who hate each other, or have no earthly idea who the other person is in the scene with you. You are also allowed to leave the stage if you think that it would be true to the moment. You can die if you are shot, you can fire a bad employee, you can ask for a divorce. If it happens in real life, it can happen onstage.

This is an important point and divergent from many of the classical improv teachings. For an audience to laugh or cry, they must care. For them to care, they must believe. If we don't behave truthfully to the moments the audience is seeing, they may stop believing, stop caring, and stop laughing. If we are afraid to walk out of a scene about a terrible first date because our improv teacher told us not to, the audience will stop believing. If the moment would compel a reasonable person to say no, ask a question, leave, or die, we must do it. Even it means "ruining" the scene.

So We Can Never Have Scenes in Fantasy Land?

No more crazy scenes? Everything must take place in our world and in our time? Not at all. Consider the Harry Potter and *Twilight* franchises. Why did one capture the imaginations of children and adults alike while the other made only slight excursions from the teen-girl market into the mainstream? They're both fantastical, but something makes Harry Potter more believable.

How important is believability? Ever see a movie or read a book you didn't like? Why didn't you like it? I frequently ask my students this question and I get answers like, "People don't talk like that," "The characters were too witty," "The hero did something out of nowhere," "Too many plot holes." If I had to throw a net over all of the reasons why we don't like certain movies or books, it would be this: we quit believing what we're seeing is real.

But Harry Potter is far from real. How are flying brooms and bubbling potions believable? Believability lies not in the circumstance or the premise but in the actions of the people involved in them. If their behavior is real, the scene will be real, regardless of how off-the-wall the scenario is. Despite being wizards, Harry, Hermione, and Ron behave like real people.

A quick note about the scene examples in this book: Their purpose is not to be funny or creative but to highlight the exercise they're being used with. They are hypothetical examples created by me and not performed by any of my students, though they are representative of the quality of play I expect. For simplicity, the characters have the same names as the actors portraying them. They are written as though they were taking place in a class. My verbal instructions to the performers and any side-coaching comments are in italics.

This is an example of the Simple Scenes exercise located in the back of this book. This exercise involves players being themselves in as much detail as possible. It is meant to give players confidence in playing slower scenes driven by character behavior rather than a strong comedic premise. This particular example involves two actors, Mary and Joe. I'll begin with my instructions:

Begin by playing the scene as close to reality as you can. Your partner will be someone you know, perhaps a friend or coworker. The scene will start very close to your actual life but as it unfolds you may discover that the character you are playing is becoming different from yourself. Go with it. Whoever wishes to speak first, the initiator, must say a line that they've said in their lives in the past week. The other player, the responder, should just give an honest reaction to what they hear. I'll stop the scene and give notes as it goes along.

> Mary (miming drinking something): I got chewed out by my boss today.
>
> Joe (seeing Mary mime a beverage, he also pantomimes a drink): Sorry to hear that.

Mary: Yeah, I'm convinced he hates me.

Joe: Must be hard to work there.

Mary: I'm stuck in an apartment I can't afford so I'm stuck with this job.

Joe: That's too bad.

Six lines in and I'm content, mostly, with what they have created. What's going on? The players probably have ideas in their heads, but to a third-party viewer – the audience – what's going on isn't very clear or detailed. We have no sets, props, or costumes in improv, so we have to be direct when providing information.

When playing a scene like this, many of my students feel pressure to make something happen, perhaps revealing that Mary killed her boss or that Joe is the boss in disguise. Before we start inventing absurd situations for these people, though, let's refine what we already have. We know they're friends, or at least friendly toward each other. We know they're drinking something. Not much, but it's a fine place to start.

Are you two friends sharing a drink? Where are you? I know it's someplace casual. Say the simple, obvious thing.

Mary: Thanks for meeting me at Cup O'Coffee. I just had to get out of there.

Joe: No prob.

Mary: I think my boss intentionally sets me up to fail.

Joe: You think he'd do that?

They're at a coffee shop. Perfect. Coffee shop is no better than break room, tavern, or out back by the Dumpsters. It's a simple answer that grew from what we already knew. Due to its clarity and mundane nature, it's a very strong answer, one that is easy to play. Remember, this exercise is about attacking reality head-on. This is not the time to get creative by putting them on the moon or making them ants in an anthill bar.

What else do we know about the scene? Joe hasn't really said very much. His lack of action, whether caused by fear on the actor's part or made as a calculated choice, is what the audience sees and must be played as though it were a choice. Perhaps it suggests that he's not as good a friend to Mary as she thinks. This may not be Joe's intention – in his mind he may think he's her longtime boyfriend – but his actions don't show that. The audience can't see inside his brain. What they can see are his polite, non-committal answers. Mary needs to see them, too.

Mary, how has Joe been behaving?

Mary: Bad day at work too? You haven't said much.

Joe: Not really. Just a long day.

I don't care if a player says no, asks questions, or just stands there without providing information, as long as their partner recognizes it and plays it as a choice. Asking questions, saying no, and being stone-faced are part of life, and if they happen onstage they are now the truth of that moment. (Many "bad" improv moves can easily be fixed by the scene partner addressing the moves as choices made by the partner's character).

This is a real pivot moment for Joe. He needs to decide which of the several possible realities is going on. He needs to decide which scene he wants to be playing. The two most obvious possibilities for Joe are (a) "I'm truly concerned about Mary and I just happen to be quiet right now" or (b) "I don't care about Mary, I'm not sure why I even agreed to come here, and I'm quiet because I wish she'd shut up." Both these realities fit the scene we've seen so far, and therefore are both equally correct. Either has just as much chance of succeeding and being funny as the other.

Joe, you haven't said or done very much. Are you happy to see Mary? Is this meeting a good thing or a bad thing?

> Joe (exasperated): A long day but I'm soooo glad to be here.

> Mary: You remember Janine? My boss set a trap for her one time.

> Joe (keenly interested): No way! Janine is an angel.

> Mary: She wouldn't hurt a fly.

> Joe: Wow, your boss must be a real bastard.

Joe has decided to be Mary's friend. Fine. He could have also played it as though meeting her was a favor. You might say he started by being quiet and is now more intense, which means that he's deviated from his original choices. Sure. But this early in the scene it is more important that Mary and Joe agree upon the context of their scene. The audience will quickly forgive the breaking of a rule no one has ever told them about if the scene bears fruit. (See Assumption 2 for more on this point.) Sometimes you have to double back to get on the right path. From here on, however, Joe must play this new choice fully.

What else do we know? We know Mary has a job and, in her opinion, a terrible boss. I say "in her opinion" because we don't know the truth. The jury – the audience – has not been presented with enough evidence. Are we seeing a slacker who was rightly yelled at or are we seeing the innocent victim of an abusive manager? Given what we've seen, we can't say for sure.

Now Mary is at a pivot point. She has been playing close to her personal life but now has an opportunity to play a character different from herself. She needs to choose which scene we're seeing and provide evidence so we'll see it too.

What happened at the office? Specifically. Are you a screw-up or is your boss a jerk?

> Mary: He tells me that he's really disappointed in my work and to try harder.

> Joe: Really? That's stupid.

> Mary: I know. I work very hard. I do all of my reports.

Mary isn't being detailed enough. I'm still not sure if her boss is mean or if she's a lousy employee. Both Marys would say they do their reports.

This can be a scary place for players. They worry that if they go too bold they might break something. If you go wacky-bold, then yes, maybe you

24

could break something. If you go reasonably bold, staying tightly in the world of absurd-yet-human behavior, you'll always push the scene forward.

Not detailed enough! Go there! Tell us specifically what happened so we can form an opinion of the kind of people you two are. Nothing you say is incorrect. I don't have an answer key.

> Mary: So he calls me into his office to tell me that I was late today. Duh? Like I need him to tell me that. So then he says that Carol couldn't find me to get the Q3 numbers for her report, which I am now learning was due in Houston at 8 a.m.

> Joe: If it was so important, why didn't Carol just do the math for the Q3 numbers herself?

> Mary: That's what I said, and Mr. Sellers fah-*lipped!* He says all I do is give my work to other people. He said he'd even be okay with all my personal calls if I'd at least do them at my desk so people could find me.

> Joe: He doesn't get you, Mary. You're too important for First Bank. You're an artist.

Great details. Sure, it's just a bunch of business jargon, but it provides a window into the deeper reality. Mary is a screw-up and Joe is her pity-party buddy. They've arrived at a simple, reasonable context that can be played indefinitely. The actors and the audience all see the scene in the exact same way, opening the door to humor. This scene found some absurdity, but it is certainly within the boundaries of life. People like this exist, and if we portray them honestly, we're improvising well.

That's the simplest type of scene, but it's not always easy. By doing this exercise, focusing simply on being real, and truly noticing and reacting to your partner's behavior, players learn the powerful lesson that if they give themselves a strong base in reality, the scene will always have a place to go without having to invent funny things to say. When a scene is grounded in reality, it's easy to see what else is probably true. The details presented toward the end of this scene represent one "probably true" reality. These details that make it real, unique, and – if played well – funny.

We Don't Perform Scenes, We Portray the Lives of Others

If you've taken improv classes before, you've probably heard the expression "Play the moment." I use it in my teaching. I shout it at my students when I see them playing their scenes not as characters living but as improvisers improvising. That note is usually followed by this comment: "You're not onstage with your scene partner, you're at home with your girlfriend." or "That's not your scene partner, it's some weird guy at the bus stop trying to talk to you." I don't want people to consider what the rules of improv want them to do. I want them to play the reality of the moment.

What is a moment? Moments exist whenever two people are onstage together and are defined by everything that has come prior. These moments change as more information is learned about each of the characters. This information isn't simply created by dialogue. It's created by actions, vocal tone, facial

26

expressions, and physical posture. The audience sees and is affected by all those things, whether it's a conscious choice on our part as improvisers or not.

We must see these things, too, and play our scenes not from our internal perception of what is happening, or what we wish were happening, but from what's actually happening in each moment, communicated through words, voice, face, and body.

ASSUMPTION 2:

The audience would rather a scene or show start slow and end strong than start strong and end slow.

Chicago's Navy Pier sticks out more than a half mile into Lake Michigan, and because of its midway games, restaurants, and theaters is a popular tourist destination. One of its most popular (and certainly most visible) attractions is its Ferris wheel. On warm summer nights, there's always a line, and people may wait 15 or 20 minutes for this unique view of the city's skyline.

What if there was never a line to buy tickets? What if you could just walk right on and ride? Sounds great, but what if after you got off they made you stand around for 20 minutes? How many people would choose not to ride if the wait was moved to the end of the experience?

Maybe it's our culture, or maybe it's in our DNA, but we seem to be programmed to think that the waiting comes first. A restaurant asks you to wait before your food comes. In fact, people are willing to wait 15 minutes for the food but will become agitated if they have to wait more than a few minutes for the check once they're done eating. For that matter, restaurants that bring your food out immediately (i.e., fast food) have a reputation for poor quality.

This notion of when we are and aren't willing to wait is relevant to the entertainment world. We will recommend a movie or book that starts slow and ends strong but not one that begins well and then drags painfully to its conclusion. An improv audience feels the same way. They'll give us time to figure things out. We just need to figure things out and then give them a strong scene.

Despite this, many improv exercises, including some in this book, focus on the beginnings of improv scenes, and by doing so place emphasis on that part of the scene. Players are generally more nervous about the first five lines of a scene than they are about playing the remaining 50 lines. They feel they need to be funny or at least interesting immediately.

Instead, we should take comfort in the audience's goodwill and patience. We don't have to be funny or brilliant right away. They aren't expecting it. We do need to move with purpose, observe our partner's choices, and try to build something together; the good news is that we have time to do it. Missteps and misunderstandings are easily repaired by patient players and forgiven by our patiently waiting audiences.

You don't need a funny first line or funny response to have a successful scene.

Initiating Scenes

Typically the first thing that happens in an improv scene is that someone speaks. That person is called the initiator. There's a lot of advice in other books and on the Internet about how to start an improv scene. Here are some examples:

-Say something about yourself, but make it devoid of plot:

> Meg: I'm a burger-and-fries kinda girl. Keep it simple. Keep it real.

-Say something about the other person, devoid of plot:

> Meg: I really wish you'd iron your shirts before you put them on.

-Pantomime a physical activity and talk about it:

> Meg (opening oven door): The cake is ready!

-Pantomime a physical activity while talking about something else:

> Meg (cleaning windows): I saw Jerome at the school picnic on Saturday.

-Pantomime a physical activity without saying anything:

> Meg (sweeping floor): ...

-Lay out the plot or premise (I call this a "follow me" initiation):

> Meg: Madame President, the Russian prime minister is here and you've got Cheeto goo on your face.

-Lay out the situation and also make an emotional choice that shows how you feel about it:

> Meg: All right! Enough of the horseplay, kids!

-Start with a big emotion, devoid of context:

> Meg (crying): Why? Why? Why!?!

Which one is best? The truth is that none of them will guarantee a better scene than any other. Many people put emphasis on the beginnings of scenes and feel that a poor start is the tallest hurdle for a scene to clear. I don't think that the initiator has that much power. I've seen too many scenes succeed when the initiation should supposedly have led to failure.

Assumption 2 tells us that you don't need to say anything funny at the top to have a successful scene. By extension, if players are willing to play slowly (i.e., they're not desperate for a laugh or visibly nervous), then any initiation will do.

But seriously, which way to start a scene is the best? If you spend some time playing with each of the above techniques, you'll see that the types of scenes they birth are quite different. How you start a scene has less to do with determining its success and more to do with determining its pace, mood, and what techniques you'll need to continue playing it.

So how should you start your scene? Well, what kind of scene do you want to have? Slow and moody or wacky and high-energy? The style you wish to play in determines the techniques you need to use.

Many forms ask the players to play a certain style. As a student at the iO Theater, my class graduation project was a form called Prism. It required a long, patient scene at the beginning, so we played with smaller, plot-free, more personal initiations to breed slow, relationship-exploring scenes. The middle section of the same form asked the players to make pointed comments about the long scenes that opened the show. To accomplish this, we had to play with direct, plot-heavy, "follow me" initiations. The show's last segment asked the players to be open to any kind of inspiration. If a player was inspired by a mood or notion they would initiate a scene lightly. If a player was inspired to create a specific, hopefully humorous circumstance, they would have to initiate aggressively so that their partner would understand what they had in mind.

Scenes Don't Always Start With the First Line

Do you have to actually speak to be the initiator? What if someone starts a scene by sitting and quietly laughing to themselves? That's a clear choice and could certainly be the initiation. What if the first actor onstage doesn't say anything and just stands there checking his watch while the next actor walks in and says "The doctor will see you now." Who initiated that scene? Perhaps rather than thinking that the initiator is who speaks first, we should think about who made the first move that defined and shaped the moment, the move that can't easily be ignored.

I call this a move of consequence. Longer scenes often consist of several smaller scenes, begun with a move of consequence, played one after the other without any breaks in between. Plays like *Waiting for Godot* or *True West* don't change location or jump through time (much) and are essentially one long conversation, but they can still be broken down into scenes, each beginning with a move of consequence.

Responding

If someone initiates and is therefore the initiator, the person that speaks second is called the responder. " As with initiations, there's a lot of advice floating around about the proper way to respond to initiations, and, again, they are all correct techniques. What all good responses have in common is this: they find value in the initiation.

How does a person in real life show that what they've heard is important? They react to it emotionally. That's what a good responder must do. Your character could be confused, happy, bored, titillated, or sad. The initiating line could be the best thing you've ever heard, the worst, or anything in between. It doesn't matter. Your reaction could be a huge, loud, stop-the-presses moment or a small smile and giggle. Assumption 2 reminds us that humor is secondary at this point.

Don't assume that the value is always positive to your character: the value you find could be horrifying. The key to finding value is in making a simple and clear choice – any choice – about how you feel about the line or situation your partner is setting up. Don't over-think this. In fact, don't think at all. Just make a choice and go with it.

> **"Wow, what you just said is really important"**...
> is not an emotion. It doesn't count. Neither does being hungry or tired, or having a broken arm, or being sick. A sick person who insists on coming to work despite bleeding out of their eyes could make for a fun character, but simply being sick – something totally out of someone's control, and something that could be accompanied by any emotion – is not enough.

Let's pretend you're eating lunch in the office break room. You feel someone standing behind you. You turn around and you see ...? Your reaction will be one of two things: "Oh, good, it's someone I like" or "Oh, yuck, it's someone I don't like." It's impossible to not have a feeling.

This emotional reaction is the first thing that takes place in all our daily interactions. It even happens with strangers. True story: When I got a library card, the first line of my "scene" with the lady behind the counter was her asking me, quite politely, "May I help you?" My response, happy to see how pleasant she was, was "Ah! Yes. I need a library card."

If she had ignored me when I approached the counter, typing away at her computer instead of acknowledging me, my response would have probably reflected the confusion I felt and the fear I had that I was disturbing her: "Ummm, excuse me...". We do it in life, so do it onstage.

It's Time to Stop Caring and Stop Listening

There is some traditional improv training that says you should always care about what's going on. But "caring" need only refer to the actor showing concern for what is going on. The character is not mandated to love or have affection for the circumstance they find themselves in. To care simply means that what is going on (good, bad, tragic, frustrating) is worthy of your character's attention. If your character didn't care about what was going on, they'd ignore it or leave. We do it in life, so we should do it onstage.

Here's a fun secret experiment to try during a rehearsal scene: as a responder, ignore your partner's first few lines, Make them get your attention. Your scene will be fine (and probably nicely textured!) as long as you and your partner play the truth that yes, your character has chosen to ignore the other person. If you're worried about denying your partner, or arguing or playing negative, table that feeling – I'll discuss that pointedly in the next section.

The Emotional Noise exercise (found in the back of this book) asks students to make emotional choices, signifying them not with words ("I'm sad" or "That makes me happy") but with emotional sounds. My setup for the exercise, as well as my side-coaching notes, appear in italics.

Barry, you will initiate this scene with a simple line of dialogue that a normal person might say in the course of their day. Less "The dog is on fire!" and more "Here are those reports you wanted." Christie, you will respond, but before you can say any clever lines of dialogue, you must give an emotional noise that conveys how you feel about hearing that line from Barry. It could be a laugh, a snicker, an oh, an ah, or an exclamation like "Damn," "All right!", "Huh?", or "Noooo!" After making that noise you may say a line of dialogue if you like. Then the scene will continue normally. No one has to make another noise in the scene if they don't want to.

Barry (pleasantly excited): You see Joey's new car?

Christie (sighs deeply): Yes, Barry. I did.

Barry (confused): So you liked it? Or you didn't?

Christie (after shallow breath): How do you think I feel? My husband bought a candy-apple-red Corvette.

Christie's noise told us a lot, much more in than her dialogue did, in fact. The deep sigh said she knows about the new car and its existence frustrates her. Barry also did a nice job of reacting to Christie's emotion. While her simple words ("Yes, Barry. I did.") didn't say much, her emotion told Barry that she's unhappy. This confused Barry, just as in life we're confused when words and emotion don't perfectly line up. With Christie's next line, we learn explicitly why she's upset. That discovery could take longer to coax out, but it's also fine to get it out early.

It's time to learn what kind of guy Barry is.

Barry. Do you understand her negative feelings?

Barry: I'm sure he'll let you ride in it.

Christie: That's not what upsets me, Barry!

Barry: Is it that it cost $90,000?

Christie: That's a good place to start.

Barry: And that it represents a happiness that you can't give him?

Christie (agitated): Why are you here, Barry?

Barry (sheepish): Joey said he'd give me a ride in his new Corvette.

Barry is an idiot. Let's hope Barry the actor recognizes that the line "I'm sure he'll let you ride in it" makes him an idiot. I'm sure that line would get a laugh, but it also defines Barry's developing pattern of behavior. It's the job of Barry the actor to recognize this and stick with it.

Christie, I want to know more about your relationship with Joey. Keep it simple. Please avoid saying that he bought it with drug money.

>Christie: You know we never had a honeymoon? The kids are finally old enough for us to leave them at home and he goes and buys a penis on wheels.
>
>Barry: I can come back another time ...
>
>Christie: No, Barry, you're staying. I need to vent. You know where Joey told me he was going last weekend when he was actually buying this car?
>
>Barry: Um .... he said that he was going to visit his aunt in Lexington?
>
>Christie: (surprised) Yes. How did you know?
>
>Barry (embarrassed): I was with him.

We've got a super awkward situation here. Rather than trying to be funny, Christie went simple with what is probably true (we never had a honeymoon) as opposed to what fanciful thing could be true (he bought the car with drug money) . There will be plenty of time to be creative later; for now let's just play the simple reality that presents itself.

As the scene plays out it becomes a simple scene: two characters living their lives truthfully. And as I discussed earlier, emotional reactions are the start of every natural moment in our lives. The emotional noise exercise forces the players to make a clear emotional choice. Since it's how conversations begin in our lives, making emotional choices in our improv scenes will push them forward.

It's Completely Outside My Control

Be careful about inventing reasons for why your actions are out of your control: "I'm sorry I moved your car. A policeman told me that he was going to ticket it," or "Yes, I used your computer to print out that report because our boss threatened to fire us if I didn't." Don't blame an outside force of higher status. You did whatever you did because of a flaw in your moral character that you're either proud or ashamed of. Playing chess is what I call when two players refuse to take personal responsibility for their circumstances:

"I only stole that money from your purse to pay for the gas bill that you forgot to pay."

"Don't you remember when we changed the bills to your name?"

"Yes I do, but you didn't put your share in the money envelope on the fridge."

"You never said which fridge. My money is in an envelope on the basement mini-fridge."

"You mean the one we sold yesterday at the garage sale?"

Etc... forever and ever.

The above scene would have been very different if Christie had reacted with any of the following emotional noises and lines of dialogue:

Barry (pleasantly excited): You see Joey's new car?

Christie (very excited, squeal with happiness): Oh boy, did I!

or

Christie (cries quietly to herself, pointing offstage): You mean that one?

or

Christie (gives an an excited, sexually tinged giggle): I have not. Yet. Yet!

or

Christie (crosses arms and gives a "Harrumph!"): I guess I'm the last to know about everything.

Each of those reactions and lines would result in very different scenes. Which one is more right or more funny? They're all equally good and each has just as much chance of succeeding as the others.

This illustrates just how powerful the responder can be. Perhaps Barry had a much bigger scene idea in mind when he initiated, but he's had to drop it and play the moment with Christie. We think of the initiator as having the power but the same initiation resulted in five very different scene starts.

This exercise reveals an important truth about relationship scenes: they aren't about *what* is going on but about *who* is going on. The above scene isn't about a new car or an inconsiderate husband, it's about an angry woman displacing her feelings onto a mostly innocent guy. If you were sitting on a park bench and you saw this scene happen, you'd laugh (to yourself). Relationship scenes are not about clever premises; they're about the friction between people behaving honestly. They de-emphasize the *what*. They are born not from words or clever initiations but from simple emotional reactions.

Whatever You Do, Don't Yes-And

Should the responder make a big emotional noise in every scene they're in? Perhaps not. Assume a player purposefully takes the stage and gives an intricate follow-me-type initiation. As the responder, you may not be sure what they're going for, but you certainly know they have something very particular in mind. I would recommend yessing without and-ing in these situations. Say "yes" lines like "Okay," "Sure," or "So that's why I'm here?" until you understand what your partner is going for. (It might take a couple of lines.) Then you can start and-ing by adding information.

Improv scenes are much more robust than people realize. Many of my students are afraid of saying too much or of saying the wrong thing, and feel that the success or failure of a scene falls squarely on their shoulders. I tell them that if you just play the reality of the moment it's actually hard to ruin a scene.

Below are some ways to respond to your scene partner's initiation that many students are afraid to use. On first reading, they might appear to be destructive to a good improv scene. They are, however, things that happen to us in our real lives. When you try them in scenes, you'll find that they won't ruin anything. On the contrary, you may find them adding life and excitement.

- Initiate your own scene after the initiator finished (a cross initiation):

> Frank: I just got back from the grocery store and they're tearing down the pizza parlor next door.

> Lisa: Frank, the prom bus leaves in five minutes and you're not in your tuxedo.

- Cut your partner off with something off-topic before they're finished speaking:

> Frank: I just got back from the grocery store and–

> Julia: I beat Pac-Man today! On that old Atari 2600 in the basement ... kill screen!

- Cut your partner off before they're finished by objecting to what they're saying:

> Frank: I just got back from the grocery store and –

> Julia: Whoa, whoa! I told you that I wanted to do the shopping this week.

- Have a large emotional outburst before your partner finishes:

> Frank: I just got back from the grocery store and--
>
> Julia (huge laughter): Ha ha!

- Look your partner in the eye and say nothing:

> Frank: I just got back from the grocery store and they're tearing down the pizza parlor next door.
>
> Julia (direct eye contact): ...

- Ignore your partner (by honestly not hearing them or by pretending to not hear them):

> Frank: I just got back from the grocery store and they're tearing down the pizza parlor next door.
>
> Julia (not paying attention): Huh? I'm sorry, I had my headphones on.
> or
>
> Julia (artificially cheerful): Well, the grocery store. I hope you got Chex Mix.

ASSUMPTION 3:

The more deeply the audience understands a scene, the more likely they are to be emotionally affected by it.

The Ferris wheel at Navy Pier is not the oldest but Chicago can claim the worlds first Ferris wheel build in 1893. Other Chicago world's firsts include the first skyscraper, first pinball machine, and (most proudly?) first McDonald's franchise.

Just twenty miles southwest of downtown is another first: located in the quaint forest preserve of Red Gate Woods is the world's first nuclear waste dump. Buried under the ground are the remains of the world's first nuclear reactor, built in 1942 as part of the Manhattan Project.

Nuclear energy is scary. We can't see what's going on. A piece of radioactive plutonium could easily be mistaken for a lump of steel. However, when you get a bunch of plutonium in the same room together, magical things happen. Plutonium nuclei are unstable, like a bunch of wobbly block towers built by a preschooler. As one inevitably falls over, its pieces crash into another, causing *it* to fall over. Etc, etc, etc ... Hiroshima.

The cause-and-effect nature of nuclear reactions has similarities with improvisation. While nuclear reactions require fertile materials and fast-moving neutrons, our improv reactions require open minds and information.

At its most basic level, improv is information, be it words or gestures or physical actions. It's the information that moves between you and your partner that excites you and drives you to action. No action, no reaction. No pinch, no ouch. No information comes in, no information returns.

Giving information doesn't prevent your partner from giving information or steal information from them. It encourages more information. We fear giving obvious information or that our information will negate a future, fun and surprising bit of information, and yet that fear prevents the information chain reaction from happening. As improvisers, we are merchants of information. And it is the information we have that the audience pays to see and will laugh at and tell their friends about the next day at work.

The opposite of information is confusion. Has an eight-year-old child ever told you a story? It's often confusing until a parent steps in to fill in the details. Confusion is uncomfortable to an audience. Good improv is rarely confusing, and neither are really good movies or books. They may be challenging or mysterious or ambiguous, but if you aren't sure which characters are which, you probably won't enjoy the story. It's only when we understand what's going on, thanks to a ton of information, that we can begin to experience any emotion.

The best books and improv scenes don't stop at not-confusing. They push on to deep clarity. Just as confusion unsettles an audience, clarity engages them. Clarity is achieved with pointed, detailed information. In our improv scenes, details are provided by the players and, just as in life, if you're unsure of what your friend is saying or doing, you must ask questions. Questions get answers, answers are information, and information brings clarity.

Provide clear details. If your partner isn't being clear, ask them for details.

The Negative Yes

Let's revisit the scene between Mary and Joe at the coffee shop. She complains to him that her boss is giving her a hard time. At first Joe is quietly going along with Mary. Then he decides to actively be on her side. What if Joe decides that rather than being a (temporarily quiet) friend of Mary's he instead isn't fond of Mary and is only there as a favor? Here's that scene again:

> Mary: Thanks for meeting me at Cup O' Coffee. I just had to get out of there.
>
> Joe: No prob.
>
> Mary: I think my boss intentionally set me up to fail.
>
> Joe: You think he'd do that?
>
> Mary: Bad day at work too? You haven't said much.
>
> Joe: Yeah, long day.
>
> Mary: You remember Janine? My boss set a trap for her, she's been gone for months.

Joe has been quiet up until this point. In the previous example, he chose to be supportive of Mary. In this example, he decides he's not happy about meeting her.

> Joe (quietly dismissive): Bosses don't set traps for their employees, Mary. They can just transfer or fire them.

46

Mary: You haven't met Mr. Sellers. He called me lazy in front of everyone.

Joe: Mary, seriously, you're late to everything. You told me to be here at 2:00 and it's almost 3:15.

Mary: I was on my way down at like 2:15 but had to stop. New. Gossip. From. Daniel.

Joe (deep sigh): You told me on the phone, through tears, that you were going to quit and needed to see me.

Mary: Things have changed. Daniel said that Gary in accounting said that...

Joe is no longer a pity party buddy but a put-upon friend guilted into meeting with Mary. You may say Joe denied Mary by not being happy to see her. He did not. Mary's behavior in the initial part of the scene, especially with the line about her boss setting traps, could be seen as her complaining and being paranoid. Joe feels put off by a paranoid complainer, just as you or I might feel in real life. If that's the reality the audience sees, then Joe must see it, too. In fact, to *not* see Mary's behavior would be a denial.

Denial: The Misunderstood Improv Villain

On day one of a typical improv class, denial is the first thing you are told not to do. If some one says you are in an airplane, don't say, 'No, we're not, we're in bathtub." Don't tell your partner they are wrong and change the facts to what you want them to be. I was always told denial is the most egregious error one could commit; an affront to yes-and, Viola Spolin, and

47

Del Close. Yet despite it being thought of as so evil, the kind of in-your-face denial I described above rarely happens. There is a type of denial that happens much more frequently that is far more dangerous: the denial of omission.

A denial of omission is when a player doesn't use what their partner gives them. It usually happens when a player makes a choice and their partner doesn't know what to do with it, so they ignore it.

It also happens when a player makes an emotional choice – the acknowledgment of which might take the scene to an uncomfortable place – and it's ignored. Bear in mind that "uncomfortable" means something different for each player. For some people, any and all emotion is uncomfortable.

Omittive denial erodes the truth of a moment by causing confusion in the audience. They saw and heard what happened, so why didn't the other character?

The first concept that really shook me when I moved to Chicago is something I call the negative yes. It involves a character taking a negative point of view about what is happening while accepting that it's occurring. When an actor takes a negative-yes position they're saying to their partner, "I agree that what you say is happening is truly happening. However, I'm not happy about it." Joe's line "Bosses don't set traps for their employees, Mary. They can just transfer or fire them" is an example of a negative yes.

Much of the traditional improv pedagogy pushes agreement, asks us to avoid conflict, and preaches that we should make our partner more important than we are. These things aren't incorrect. However, they fail to make a distinction between the potentially different motivations of the actor and the character they're portraying.

Our real lives are full of moments we're unhappy about, so why should our improv rules say those scenes aren't good enough for the stage? We should never feel forced to be happy about getting fired or to agree that it would be best if we got divorced. To look at it another way, if a player is intentionally trying to be annoying or stupid and their partner accommodates the annoying behavior, it's a denial.

In our lives we purposefully accommodate certain "odd" behaviors of others because we don't want them to stand out – we want the behaviors to be perceived as normal. Our friend who has a stutter. Our boss who walks funny due to an old injury. Our grandmother who's hard of hearing. We intentionally gloss over these strange behaviors because we care about the people. We don't want them to feel out of place. However, in an improv scene we put on behaviors because we want them to be noticed: we're *trying* to be out of place. Accommodating in an improv scene can erase choices of absurdity.

Here's an example to illustrate the notion of negative yes. These are the first two lines of a scene:

Liz (pantomiming being at a school locker): ...

Terrance (big smile, rocking on his feet, holding pantomimed books across his chest): Great game last Friday. You're an amazing volleyball player, but I'm sure you've heard that. I'm sure you know the big dance is coming up and I was wondering...

Simple scene, yes? A fairly wordy follow-me initiation but still simple: real people in a recognizable situation. Liz is about to be asked to the big high school dance.

What are Liz's options? Is it a denial or bad form to not accept Terrance's invitation to the dance? The answer is found yet again in real human behavior. Whatever her options would be in life, those are her options onstage.

She could very well give a big laugh, slam her locker, and walk away. That would be a short scene, but it's not automatically a bad scene. It may not even be over when she leaves. Who's to say we couldn't watch Terrance cry for a few moments by himself before being joined by his nerdy friends? Couldn't you see that happening in a TV show? If it can happen in a TV show, or a movie, or a play, or in life, it should be able to happen in an improv scene.

Remember the example of someone walking up behind you in the office break room? You're either cool with them disturbing you or uncool with them disturbing you. Similarly, all of Liz's possible lines will place the scene in one of two worlds. One world is "I'm cool with what's happening." The other world is "I'm not cool with what's happening." In class, I use the shorthand phrases "playing with" and "playing against." Let's explore those options in more depth.

The choice of Liz being cool with Terrance 's dance proposal – "playing with" him – could take many forms. Here are a few:

Liz (nervous and giddy): ... if I want to go with you? Sure! I mean yes. Wait, were you going to ask me to the dance?!?

Liz (calm and cool): Go on. You wanted to ask me out? Okay, I'll rock the dance with you.

Liz (polite): If you could take me to the dance? Sounds great. Thanks, Terrance.

Liz (nervous and reserved): Gulp!... um, yeah, I heard about the dance. You, um, uh, asked anyone yet?

Liz (confident): Yes! (big hug)

Those are five reasonable responses among the million or so responses that live in the "I'm cool" pool. Here are some "I'm not cool" or "playing against" choices:

Liz (a bit surprised but calm): Oh gosh, Terrance, I'm sorry. You're a very nice guy but I'm already going with Jack. Maybe I'll see you there.

Liz (stonefaced): You talking to me? You know you're standing in the nerd exclusion zone, right?

Liz (without making eye contact): Yeah, I've got this thing that night. Real busy. Really busy.

Liz (evil grin): Me? Liz "Rock Star" McGee, go to the dance with you, Terrance "Dorkzilla" Cole?

Liz (pleasant but disappointed): Terrance, you can't keep doing this. I'm flattered but I'm still dating Jack, just like for the last eight months. I thought we talked about you asking Penelope.

Which of those ten choices above will result in the best scene? The truth is that the "I'm not cool" scenes have as much as a chance of success as the

"I'm cool" scenes. Even though I say you have only two options, you can see that you actually have infinite options that fall into two categories. Improvisers only get into trouble when they don't commit to their response or when they try to switch categories mid-scene.

That's not to say that you can't switch reactions, but it's a challenging move. The impulse to switch may come from fear of having taken on what feels like an unplayable position, from growing discomfort with being negative, or from the boredom of being nice. Changing points of view also comes from players trying to be funny, and while a single line might be rippingly hilarious, going against earlier choices endangers the long-term viability of the scene.

Real people do change their points of view, but as with someone who's discovered religion or vegetarianism later in life, the changes are fervent choices. If Liz originally doesn't want to go out with Terrance but then decides to, it wouldn't be as a lark. She'd have to be worn down, and even then she might have an ulterior motive – perhaps pity, or something *Carrie*-esque.

This notion of being cool and uncool is explored in the exercise With and Against found in the back of this book.

Please Understand That I Don't Understand
There is a third choice. It is to be willfully oblivious to what's going on. By "willful," I mean that the actor is choosing to play a character so stupid or so unable to read the actions of others that they have no idea what's going on. My favorite example is the pool boy and the sexually aggressive housewife.

Clyde: Well, the pool's clean, Mrs. Taylor. Can I put my shirt back on?

Mrs. Taylor (slinking around sexually): Leave it off, Clyde, I still have some work for you to do. Up in the bedroom.

Clyde: Another light bulb needs changing? I must have changed every bulb up there four or five times ...

Mrs. Taylor: Shut up. No light bulbs. A spider. In my shower. I want you to kill it.

Clyde: Okay.

Mrs. Taylor: Have you ever been with a woman before?

Clyde: Um .... where?

Clyde is an idiot. Beyond being polite, he is neither cool or uncool with what's really happening, because he doesn't see what's really happening. This is a fun choice to play but it must be played as a choice. A player can't decide halfway through a scene it would be funny to start playing dumb. From line one, you must communicate that you are oblivious to what's going on.

Characters

The simple scenes I described at the beginning of this section, where actors play as reasonable people would in life, represent a sound way to play that is, generally, never incorrect. However, allowing scenes to emerge from a grounded reality is not the first thing people think of when they think of improv comedy. They think of fantastical and improbable situations. They think of ridiculous characters.

What is a character? What isn't a character? Do characters need funny walks or silly voices? Do they have to be larger than life? How close to yourself can you play before you stop being a character? When we say a fellow improviser is great at playing characters, what is it exactly that they are doing to make us say that?

Many of the established techniques for creating characters involve concepts like motivations and emotional memory. Many techniques are rather intricate, so intricate that while they may be fine as analytical tools, they're too involved to be useful during an actual improv scene. Improv is immediate and our working definition of "character" needs to be simple and easily implemented. Like every other lesson so far in this book, our definition of character comes from the characters we meet in our everyday lives.

Think of a person in your life who makes you mad. Consistently. Do you have them in mind? Describe their behavior with a few specific words. The fewer the better. Avoid generalities like mean, stupid, a jerk, horrible, or irritating. Instead, describe the specific behavior that gets under your skin: talks too much, incompetent at their job, sexually forward, a know-it-all, refuses to respect personal boundaries, nauseatingly happy.

None of those attributes are criminal offenses or even exceptionally wacky. They are real and rather common. Most importantly, they're specific. They are also serial behaviors. The person who does them does them all the time. We can call these behaviors absurd, not because they are totally off the wall, but because compared to the reality we live in, they stick out. These repeatedly performed absurd attributes form a pattern of behavior. These behavior patterns comprise half of our definition of character. We need something additional to make these absurd points of view useful in our improv scenes.

Let's get back to the person you thought of who makes you mad. Why are they still in your life? Why don't you run away every time you see them? Because they're your coworker and you need your job. They're your classmate and you can't drop the class. They're a friend of your friend and you like your friend. They're the DMV clerk and you need to get your driver's license renewed. There's a simple, real-world reason that forces you to interact with them. Characters can't operate in a vacuum, and this fact is missed by most of the character-building tools actors and improvisers are taught.

Our character definition consists of both a behavioral component and a contextual component. If you come across a person who talks too much and you don't need to interact with them, you won't. If a guy at a bar who isn't a friend of your best friend is inappropriately forward sexually, you flick them off and walk away. Tension is only created when two forces are in opposition. If one force is nonexistent or refuses to resist, there is no tension.

Think of it in terms of a hammer and an anvil: The annoying trait is the hammer, the reason that keeps you in the presence of the annoying character is the anvil, and you are the iron bar between them, getting whacked. Without the anvil's resistance, the hammer blows are ineffective.

I often see improvisers make large, ridiculous choices in an effort to create an interesting character, but the scene doesn't work because they never told us why this off-the-wall person is important to their scene partner. Some examples of characters who exhibit both behavior and context components are the incompetent dentist, the gossipy aunt, and the constantly-joking police officer. I use the adjective-plus-noun phrase for this behavior/context definition because it mirrors its purpose: you must have a consistent behavior but you must also fill a role in the lives of your scene partners, forcing them to interact with you.

You Yourself Are a Character

You're a character, too, if you behave in a consistent manner and fill a needed role in your scene. Absurdity is not required. You are the straight man, living truthfully in an imaginary world. To be a good straight man, you need to be to be able to do two things: react truthfully to the potentially weird things around you and behave consistently. Believe me when I say the straight man has all the power in the scene.

The following is an example of the Behavior/Context Character Exercise[1] from the back of

---

[1] I used to call this exercise The Clingy Priest. Old students of mine may recognize it by that name. I in no way meant to imply inappropriate touching or sexual misconduct by members of the clergy. When I developed this exercise the first example I thought of was of an overly-friendly, platonic minister who loves hugs and giving shoulder rubs. I called it The Clingy Priest and the name stuck.

this book. This exercise is good for leading actors to make strong, playable choices so they can gain experience playing improvised characters. It's also good for generating a type of scene game called the frustration game. (More on scene games later.)

Before the exercise I prepare two piles of paper slips. In one pile are written behaviors, while the other pile contains contexts. This example involves two actors, Claire and Doug. Here are my instructions:

One of you will draw one slip from each pile. Together they form a random character. Do not tell your partner what you drew. (In this case Doug drew "talks too much" and "bank teller.") You will also initiate the scene. The responder will not draw any slips and play this scene as a normal person— the straight man — and live truthfully in the simple moment. Remember, whatever weird things happen in this scene are truly happening in the life of the rational person you are portraying.

> Doug (Cheerful): Welcome to Community Bank, how may I help you?
>
> Claire: Yes, I have a–
>
> Doug: Don't tell me! You're here to make a deposit. Work check? Personal?
>
> Claire (a bit taken aback): Um, yes. I'm here to deposit a check.
>
> Doug: Is it a ...?
>
> Claire: It's a work check.
>
> Doug: That was my next question! Are you a mind reader? What number am I thinking of? I

bet you hope it's your account number!

Claire (calm and matter-of-fact): I'm not a mind reader, I just want to deposit my check.

Doug: Are you sure? Maybe I'm the mind reader?

Claire (still calm): Wow, that would be cool.

OK, so far so good. Doug is certainly a bank teller; he was very clear up top. If we don't know what's going on, we can never have a scene. He's also talking far too much for a typical bank transaction. Claire is being a bit accommodating. Not playing fully against but also not really playing with. No change in emotion, just rolling with Doug's weirdness. In this exercise I would like Claire to play against. It's most likely Doug's intention that she play against him and not think he's the funniest person ever.

Doug, if she's not saying "ouch," you need to pinch harder. Claire, if you're pinched, say "ouch."

Doug (still very merry): Let's see what we have here. Let me just begin the process by typing your name into my computer. Ah! I see you're low on the ol' fundage, good thing you want to make a deposit.

Claire (perturbed): I'd appreciate it if you didn't make remarks about my account information.

Doug: Sorry, ma'am, it's part of my job.

Claire: Part of your job is commenting on my balance?

Doug: Nope, that's a free service ...
Claire (gives an angry look): ...

Doug: You're right, on to your check. Wow, a big one! Let's take this to Vegas.

Claire (terse, taking care to look at name tag): Look, Doug, I don't have a lot of time. If we can just hurry this along.

Doug has ramped up the annoying – perfect. Claire is standing up for herself – very nice. If someone says or does something stupid, it is your job to mention it. Claire, as the straight person, represents the audience's point of view. We see ourselves in her situation and empathize with her. She must keep the audience trusting her.

Claire, why are you in a hurry? Keep it simple.

Doug (face down, typing away): Not much longer, ma'am. Just another moment. *Un momento. Prego! Una moneta,* huh!

Claire (angry): I have only thirty minutes for my lunch break. If you can't handle a simple transaction ... the teller next to you is vacant, I'm going over there.

Ah, the anvil! She's on her lunch break and doesn't have much time. Completely reasonable.
While "I'm on the run from the Mafia" and "I'm actually robbing this bank" seem funny and sexy, they are complex choices to play. Besides, the simple reality that exists is interesting. No one in the audience has probably ever robbed a bank, but they have deposited checks and they have dealt with people like Doug. They

can relate to this scene.

Claire, say the problem you are having with Doug. Doug, you're pushing very hard. Do you want her to leave?

Doug (sensing he's losing her): I'm sorry, miss. I really love my job and helping people.

Claire (calmer, but still firm): You talk entirely too much. I suggest you get moving on my transaction without the side comments.

Doug: Certainly, ma'am. I have been told that I can be a bit loquacious.

Claire: (stonefaced): ...

Doug (quiet, face down in his work): I'll print out a receipt with your present balance.

Claire: (stonefaced) ...

Doug: Your new balance will take effect at 2 AM this evening.

Claire: (stonefaced): ...

Doug: Loquacious means I talk too much.

Claire: (flips out): I know what it means!!!

If played well this scene could continue for many minutes. Claire must play it real, and as long as Doug doesn't push too hard, it could continue indefinitely. He just needs to keep drawing her back in. It's easy to create tension in your scenes. You'll earn your paycheck not by creating tension but by managing it, drawing it out, and playing it moment to moment as it would unfold in real life.

Sometimes players cling too tightly to their absurdity. They feel that if they aren't behaving in their absurd fashion at every moment, they're doing it wrong. Actually, the opposite is true. Players must learn to give in and lose. If Claire insists on seeing a manager, a real-life Doug might "lose" by taking Claire seriously for just a moment rather than lose his job. Doug wouldn't be going against his earlier choices; he'd be adding depth to his character.

Maniacs vs. Serial Killers

Maniacs and serial killers aren't the same. Maniacs go on crazy stabbing rampages and can't be talked out of it. Serial killers are smart. They are calculating and very much in control of themselves ... in addition to be a terrifying and unwelcome part of our society. When a serial killer is afraid of being caught or found out, they might "hide the knife" so they won't be seen as a killer. "What? A knife? No, no, don't be ridiculous. Now please, let me give you a ride in my van."

The maniac analogy fits players who play the frustrating character too hard. Temporarily relenting on the behavior doesn't undo the character any more than a serial killer not stabbing someone at all times means they don't want to.

If your scene reaches an impasse – "I want to go out for dinner" vs. "We should eat in" – one side must lose, but they must not change their point of view. It might look like this: "Fine! We'll eat in. Whatever." Or "Okay, if you want to spend more money we don't have, we'll eat out." Both of those responses begrudgingly concede the argument but their opinion about what would be best – eating in or eating out – has not changed. An example of losing *and* giving up your point of view looks like this: "Oh, I see. Yes, you are right. We should eat in." (though it might work if it were sarcastic!)

But Bill Said We Could Argue

Yes, these scenes may feature arguing. Sorry. Arguing happens in life, in books, and in plays. Some of our favorite scenes from movies are arguments. "Luke, I'm your father." "That's impossible!" I would prefer to not categorically forbid huge parts of our human existence from the improv stage.

There are, however, a few truths about arguing that can cause trouble. Most importantly, characters may argue; actors may not.

Actors need to accept the unpleasant realities and not deny that they exist. Also, an argument between two characters with reasonable points of view is a debate, and unless the viewer has a stake in one of the points of view, it could be boring.

An example of a debate scene might be a boy who wants to leave the farm and move to the big city while his family wants him to stay because the farm needs his help. A reasonable person can see both sides. Good argument scenes feature a reasonable point of view colliding with an unreasonable point of view.

Inside Out and Outside In

To be an improviser you must accept the fact that you are first an actor. It's easy to get lost in the wit and clever dialogue of improv and forget that our scenes are being created by live people in front of live people. The audience won't believe or be affected by what they see if we're not effectively communicating it. Standing around hoping to think of funny things to say is a dead-end street. But before you rush to take an acting class, know this: Western society has already equipped you and me with a catalog of easy and effective characters to portray.

The Behavior/Context character exercise (talkative bank teller was the example) only asks the improviser to assume a behavior, yet whenever I run it in class, improvisers accentuate their behaviors with physical and vocal choices. I hesitate to label these physical and vocal characterizations as conscious choices. Through acculturation (or maybe even through DNA), people link attitudes with physicality.

Ask a group of actors to walk around onstage pretending to be NASA rocket scientists. I doubt many of them will poke out their guts and waddle about. Most will walk tall and awkwardly, making quick and short steps, while speaking with a stammering voice and pantomiming pushing glasses up their noses. Humanity has made these links between behavior and physicality. Perhaps it's stereotypical (or, more politely, archetypal). Similarly, actors doing the Behavior/Context exercise start with a mental choice and allow it to affect their body and voice. These choices are influenced by this system of cultural archetypes.

This may seem obvious. But the fact that we link behavior to physicality begs the question: Can we work backward and discover behaviors by first

63

adopting a specific physicality? The answer is yes.

Allow me to compress several months of acting class into one paragraph: Deciding how a character walks, for example, can be the basis for figuring out point of view. Ask an actor to walk around the stage while sticking their gut out, leaning back, and scratching their belly. Then ask them to speak in whatever voice they feel would fit that posture. Who are they? What do they do for a living? How do they spend their free time? Having done this a lot, let me say I get few NASA rocket scientists and many country-boy NASCAR fans.

Does everyone become a country-boy NASCAR fan? No, but enough do to demonstrate a link between physicality and personality. This is called working outside in, from the physical to the behavioral. Whereas the Behavior/Context exercise, and any exercises that starts with a mental choice that affects physicality and voice (e.g., I want to be a talkative bank teller), is working inside out, from your brain to your body. Ultimately, an outside-in character must have a consistent behavior and a reason for existing to be effective, but those things can be discovered over the first several lines of a scene, rather than having to be thought of before the scene begins.

Many players prefer this style of play. It breeds interesting characters that, because they are grown from the physical, are dynamic to watch and visceral in personality. Scenes played by outside-in characters also tend to be more relationship-style than game-of-the-scene style.

Many of the classic improv exercises – mirroring, imitating animals, speaking in gibberish, matching energies – force actors to both listen and create in this style. Improv isn't a game of chess to someone playing outside-in; it isn't a game at all. Rather than clever wordplay, these improvisers use their character's strong personalities to create moments. You'll find that these scenes have a very different texture from the inside-out, Behavior/Context scenes. Which do you prefer? Which scenes are needed in your show?

Audiences Don't Come To Check Your Homework

Sometimes an actor is so concerned with figuring out and honoring their own choice they don't play the moment and never make a meaningful connection with their partner. You must be alive and emotionally available to your partner. Simply making a strong choice is not improvisation; it isn't what people pay to see. This is true of all improv technique. No one tells the audience what good technique is or that they should grade you on its application. They come to see you create with your partners.

This exercise, Machine Characters, is explained in depth in the back of the book. It's designed to force players to play outside-in. The plot of the scene will not be something a player had in mind before the scene starts. Instead, the premise will grow solely from the physicality and resultant voice of the outside-in player. This exercise requires knowledge of the classic improv exercise Machine Building, in which players create rhythmic, repetitive, and cohesive "machines" using their bodies and voices to be the individual parts. I'll include a brief explanation of Machine Building with the Machine Character exercise explanation. Here's my explanation to the actors:

Three actors onstage, please. Adam, you will begin a machine as you would in a Machine Building exercise. Bethany, you are to join the machine in a complementary fashion, again, as you might in a Machine Building exercise. After Bethany has found her machine rhythm to my satisfaction, I will excuse Adam from the stage. Casper, you will take the stage, assume a neutral posture, and prepare to receive a vocal initiation from Bethany. Bethany, when you're ready you will transform your machine posture, motion, and noise into a character voice and movement. Your machine physicality IS NOT an activity or transient motion you were coincidentally making at the top of the scene. It's your physiological gesture. Perhaps it implies nervousness, lethargy, or excitement. The same is true with your machine-born vocal choice. It will influence your character's speech. That is now who you are. You will also initiate the scene. Again, the physical actions, gestures, and general presence are not to be in the text of the scene. They exist only to help you find an outside-in character.

Adam (bends deeply at the knees, waves his arms in a baseball umpires "safe!" motion and makes a low hum)

Bethany (faces Adam and bends at the waist in time with Adam's arm movements. Her arms move up and down in a chopping motion. She makes high pitched squeal)

The machine continues for 15 seconds. Adam is signaled to leave the stage. Casper enters.

Bethany (transforms her waist bending into fearful bowing. Her chopping arm motions become nervous, defensive, "Stop!" gestures. She backs away from Casper): It's not what you think. All this. This is not what you think.

66

Casper (confused): Bethany. Calm down. What's wrong?

Bethany (speaking quickly): I realize the room is a mess and certain things aren't where certain things typically are.

Casper: Where's the TV? And the sofa? You said you had a surprise for me, that I should wait upstairs....

Bethany: And you should still be up there. Things aren't ready for you, Honey.

Casper: I heard a crash and what sounded like thunder.

Bethany (no longer in a crouch but still speaking quickly and defensively. And still making nervous arm chops.): That? That!? I can explain everything. But only after it's all ready. Don't ruin your birthday surprise.

Casper: Sure. I'm sorry but I just got nervous.

Bethany: Nervous?

Casper: The banging. And electrical noise!

Bethany: Oh, yeah. Sure. Let's pretend that didn't happen.

Bethany's vocal choices and words were inspired by her physicality. For many players and theaters, this is the preferred style of play. It generates fun characters with absurd bents and chaotic scene energy.

Forms that require scenes with quick energy and immediate action can be played this way. This outside-in approach to character would work well in the first and third sections of the Prism form I described earlier. (The middle section of that same show, which requires actors to have a strong scene concept and initiate with a follow-me initiation, is more suited to inside-out play.)

Assumption 4:

An audience will enjoy a funny idea, premise, or concept when it is revealed, but their enjoyment of the rest of the scene depends on how well it is played.

Before he abandoned his family, before his lover and her children were murdered by an ax-wielding madman, before he was arrested for violating the White Slave Act, Frank Lloyd Wright was one of America's most innovative architects. He got his start in the Chicago suburb of Oak Park, and much of his early Prairie-style work is still there. Carports, family rooms, and open floor plans all trace their roots to Wright. His organic architecture and flowing internal spaces contrasted with the prevailing Victorian style: cold, endless arrays of square rooms, doors, and hallways.

(Charges were quickly dropped for the White Slave Act violation. Known as the Mann Act, the loosely-worded 1910 law snared many notable "immoral" people, including Chuck Berry, Jack Johnson, and Charlie Chaplin.)

While his style changed over the years, his keen attention to detail never left. It's easy to wave your hand around an empty piece of land and talk about flowing internal spaces, but Wright went further, perhaps too far, by designing not just the inside and outside of the house but also the furniture, light fixtures, heating vent covers, and matching gowns for the lady of the house. Control freak? Yes. Megalomaniac? Perhaps. If you ever get a chance to see his work, it's this follow-through, seeing the grand concept down to the last, that will strike you.

As improvisers, it can be easy for us to leisurely wave our hand over a scene, say a truly funny line, and feel like we've earned our check for the night. But, like

Wright, our voice – our identity – is in our follow-through.

When you step onstage you are, by definition, an actor. So act. Step one is deciding who's saying that oh-so-funny line. Step two is living in that role. See your idea from the first line to the last, always playing a person and not a disembodied narrator standing just outside of the scene, hoping the next thing you say is funny.

By playing the person emotionally involved in the funny premise, we're leveraging Assumption 1, the audience's natural appreciation for things they recognize as real. Should our idea take several lines to unfold, that's no problem, because Assumption 2 says the audience will give us the time. More time means more lines, which should mean more information. The more information that is present, according to Assumption 3, the greater chance we have to get a reaction from the audience.

Truthfully portray the person involved in the funny idea, premise, or conceit.

The Game of the Scene

The word "game" has been attached to at least five different concepts in improvisation. "Game" can refer to a short form game, a group game within a Harold, or any group exploration element used in a long form show. Some premise-based scenes are referred to as "gamey" (as opposed to scenes that are relationship-based). Finally, there's the notion that within a scene exists a conceit above the scene's simple reality that the actors are secretly playing out with each other. This last definition is called the game of the scene, and it's what this section is about.

The game of the scene can be a tricky concept. Some people give it a very narrow definition, while others see it as a quasi-"in the zone" place that magically appears in some scenes. The Behavior/Context exercise is a good exercise for generating a specific type of scene game called the frustration game, but there are others. Firstly, I'll explain the game of the scene conceptually.

Back in my college improv group we played a short form game called Scene Three Ways, also known as Replay. We'd get a suggestion from the audience and then perform a scene lasting a minute or so. Then we'd get suggestions from the audience of film genres. If the first scene was about someone buying shoes and the genre suggestions were sci-fi, western, and buddy cop movie, the players would redo the shoe salesman scene as though it was a sci-fi movie, then redo it as a western, and finally as a buddy cop movie.

Anyone who has played this game recognizes there is a tangible change in playing style between the first scene and the three replays. Before the first scene, when the suggestion is taken, the players are probably thinking, "I hope I do a good scene." They're going into the scene with the suggestion and all of the improv advice they've been exposed to: be in the moment, react emotionally, yes-and, etc.

But once the replays start, the players' focus shifts. They're less worried about the rules of improv than they are about the rules of the genre they are about to portray. They're probably going through their Rolodex of sci-fi movie bits and figuring out how to inject them into the scene. The rules of the genre trump the general improv rules. If the cop movie replay puts the shoe salesman in an interrogation room, the scene would be full of questions and "no"s, things many improvisers see as illegal, but the players in this game wouldn't think twice about it.

What happened to living in the moment and reacting emotionally? What happened to listening? They're sitting in the back seat. Right now, these players aren't improvising per se; they're playing a game called the genre game.

In our example of the bank teller scene, Claire begins the scene with no idea what's going on, so she's most likely freely improvising, just playing the moments as they come. Doug, however, has received a strong suggestion from the paper slips, and, before the scene starts, is crafting a quick scenario in his mind to get his idea started. He will give a quick "follow-me" initiation and, through his next few lines, communicate to Claire, "Hey, not sure if you've noticed, but I'm a pretty talkative bank teller. My plan is to frustrate the hell out of you. Wanna play the frustration game?"

Claire, who was at first just trying to play a good scene based on the general improv guidelines, will see this and play along. The object of the frustration game is to make one character as frustrated as possible. Despite one character saying "no" and "stop" and "I'm leaving," both characters are very willing participants.

In actuality, the players haven't wholly abandoned the rules of improv to play the game. The scene still needs some honest, emotional reactions (especially from Claire) if the audience is going to believe it. A piece of Doug and Claire is standing just outside the scene, detached and aware of the whole, making choices that forward the game, yet knowing the scene must maintain a sense of reality and integrity and not simply be a series of jokes.

The first example scene in this book is one between Mary and Joe at a coffee shop. By the end, we've learned that Mary is lazy and self-important and that Joe is her enabler, helping her make excuses. If that scene were to continue, it could easily become a scene of Mary making wilder and wilder claims and accusations about her workplace ("I got a reprimand for putting a lock on one of the stall doors in the ladies' room: 'Mary's stall only'!") while Joe keeps making more tenuous excuses for her ("I'm sure anyone could have asked you for the key whenever they wanted to use it.") If Mary and Joe are having fun and decide to continue doing this, they have found a game. Some people might call this a heightening game, and while that describes what's happening textually, I'd rather describe it by how the actors are behaving. In this scene, they're playing together. They're on the same side of the absurdity. They're playing the general agreement game.

Let's Get Serious About Being Funny

Comedy can be generated when absurdity and reality rub against each other. It's easy to see that something could be made funnier by being made more absurd, but that's not the only way to make more friction. The oft-overlooked other way is to make the real more real.

Comedy arises from the contrast

73

between absurdity and reality, not the highest absolute level of absurdity. A very small absurdity, in a carefully played reality, can go a long way. A fascist vampire shoe salesman in a land of fascist vampires is just a shoe salesman. By placing your scene in a real-world context, a slightly askew behavior will contrast greatly.

Some forms require game scenes, typically favoring follow-me initiations. A form that asks the audience to clip out newspaper articles to inspire the scenes creates an expectation in the audience that the articles they selected will appear in the scenes. The players will most likely make strong, follow-me initiations with clear references to the articles and with a game idea in mind to make sure this happens.

Not all scenes have games, though most scenes present the players with an opportunity to create a game. The game can be discovered organically, like Mary and Joe in the coffee shop, or declared by a player, like Claire and Doug at the bank.

The following are some common scene games. My goal isn't to create tight boundaries that all scenes must fit into to be "correct" or successful, but rather to demonstrate that there are many right ways to play. As long as you and your partner agree to go down the same road together, you'll be fine. With that in mind, here are some of the more well-traveled roads:

Mapping Game

A mapping scene is a game that takes the behaviors and social rules of one situation and places them in a different context. Here's an example:

Dan: I bought these pants here yesterday and wanted to return them.

Sally: Was there something wrong with them?

Dan: No, the pants are fine. I'm just not sure if they're the right pants for me.

Sally: You're worried that some better pants might come along and you'd be stuck with these?

Dan: No, it's just ... I like to do things around the house, hanging out with friends, and these pants are like, going-out party pants. We don't have much in common.

Sally: I think these pants are a great match for you. It's time to try something new. You wouldn't be here if you weren't ready to try new things.

Dan: I'm not saying I have commitment issues, it's just–

Sally: Maybe you could take a break from these pants for a while. You know, find out what you really want.

What's really going on in that scene? Is Dan retuning pants or breaking up with them? While it looks like a scene about someone returning a pair of pants, the actors are playing a game where the conceits and language of a breakup are paired with the reality of a simple business transaction.

As with all games, the actors are not playing an honest relationship scene about an item return. They have an exterior, agreed-upon agenda to inject the language and the feelings of a breakup into their simple scene. A key point is that both players are playing together.

Other mapping scenes would be using the language of a street corner drug deal in a scene in a about someone ordering at a fast food restaurant, or using the language of a first date during a police interrogation.

Genre Game

Scenes can follow the rules of an existing TV, film, or literary genre. A genre is simply a set of conventions. The conventions of a buddy cop movie, for example, include a mismatched pair of cops, an angry police chief who threatens to take the loose canon off the case, and somebody who dies one day short of retirement. If your scene puts more emphasis on following those conventions than it does on general improv scene technique, you're playing a genre game. For a genre game scene to be successful, it must include the conventions we all expect to see.

> Annie (positions a chair center stage, speaks bold and loudly): Mr. Stockton, master spy extraordinaire, how would you like to die?
>
> Ryan (sits in the chair, hands behind his back): As slowly and painfully as possible would be nice.
>
> Annie: Ha! That can be arranged. Tell me, how did you learn of my plans of world domination?
>
> Ryan: Let's just say your trusted lieutenant talks in his sleep.
>
> Annie: "His sleep"? Stanley? You had sex with Stanley?

Ryan: Among others.

Annie: I always pictured you as more of a ladies' man.

Ryan: Aren't you supposed to be explaining your plans to me before shooting a laser into my crotch?

Annie: We'll get to that. Stanley? He's a bit of a bear. Is that your thing?

Ryan: My type changes with every mission. About that plan for world domination...

Annie: ... You also said "among others." This I gotta hear!

Spectacle Game

Ever have an audience laugh when a player accidentally knocks over a chair? As I mentioned in the section on scenes, audiences don't just laugh at the content of our improv scenes; they also laugh at our performances.

Actors with large personalities, scenes in which players are forced to kiss or wrestle, scenes with pantomimed car chases – these might all get nice laughs despite being improvised "poorly." Audiences understand that since the players are making it up as they go along, certain situations that would not be funny in life might be funny in an improv show.

Imagine that a girl gets a letter from her dream college. She's so nervous she can't open it. She hands it to her mother and says, "You read it." Not at all funny in real life. Possibly funny in an improv show. The actors might recognize this and make a game out of it intentionally, each insisting that the other read the letter. The humor is solely derived from the audience enjoying the spectacle of two players trying to put the burden of making something up on each other.

I was once in a very funny scene about a group of people in an underground bunker waiting out a nuclear holocaust. Three other actors and myself stood center stage talking about how we'd been there a long time and we all had things to apologize for. A fifth actor entered stage left and began pantomiming opening a large door. The three of us noticed this and folded him into the story, saying that a fifth guy had been outside investigating the destruction above. After actor five opened the door, he began pantomiming another door, and then another, eventually pantomiming his way through an increasingly elaborate series of locks, retina scans, and alligator pits.

The audience quickly lost interest in what the dialogue was about. So did I. Once the four of us recognized that the fifth guy was doing hilarious physical comedy on the side, we decided we were actually the side dish to his main course. The spectacle of seeing a player pantomime his way through an ordeal of rope swings and urine tests is what that scene became about. The rest of us could have been offended by him upstaging us, but instead we decided to play along with the emerging spectacle game. We supported the game by talking about increasingly mundane things while number five dodged laser beams, creating a fun contrast.

The lesson isn't that you should walk into every scene and do pantomime bits. However, even the most serious player must recognize that moments of clowning, physical comedy, and unintentional misspeaking (perhaps leading to intentional misspeaking) are real and available to us as players. The audience appreciates a well-played scene and they also appreciate the spectacle of our performance.

General Agreement Game

Typically humor is created when an absurdity rubs against a reality. Can we have two absurd points of view? Yes. But these can be tricky scenes to play. One fun way to pull it off is for the actors to play the same absurd point of view. Here's an example. It begins with Steve and Valerie pantomiming mundane office tasks.

Steve: Did you see what Carol is wearing today?

Valerie: Hideous. If you're built like a corn stalk, don't dress like a corn stalk.

Steve: Thank you. At least she's a nice person. Maybe the nicest person here. Unlike Mr. Phelps.

Valerie: Did you see what *he* was wearing today?

Steve: Um, not unless you mean Shirley's lipstick!

Valerie: Whoops. That's all I'm going to say. Whoops.

Steve: Cheater's Guidebook 101: Always keep a change of clothes in your office. Just in case.

Valerie: Let me amend that, a *clean* change of clothes.

Steve: Uh oh. You're just not going to let Ted off the hook, are you?

Valerie: I know it's 4 o'clock when I can smell him walking past me. His deodorant quits at the same time every day.

Gossiping secretaries being gossipy. It isn't particularly absurd or fantastical and that's fine. The trick with general agreement scenes is that both players share the same point of view and keep pushing and adding information. There won't be a frustrated straight man to question their behavior, pull information from them, or provide them with the contrast to enable absurd behavior. As the scene goes along, might we learn that Steve and Valerie are actually quite different people? Sure, but not right now.

Sometimes players find themselves in general agreement scenes and feel their position is wrong or boring or unplayable. Our players in the gossiping secretaries scene may feel that nothing is happening or that there's no conflict and the scene is suffering because of that. Rather than introducing some arbitrary disagreement or action to complete, continue adding information. What else might these people say? Trust that these characters simply being who they are is interesting.

The Jury Needs Evidence

A common note I give students is that the jury needs evidence. If a prosecutor told a jury that the defendant is, "very mean and most certainly did the thing he's accused of" and that "if you let him go, oh boy, would more bad things happen," she won't get a guilty verdict. The jury needs evidence. "The defendant, who has robbed multiple gas stations in the past, is on videotape robbing the one in question. Not only did he flip the bird to the security camera and awkwardly try to kiss the clerk, he left a trail of Doritos cheese-goo fingerprints on the counter, the bathroom doorknob, and the clerk's shirt."

Avoid vague accusations and sweeping generalizations. It's perfectly okay that your scene partner "always does that," but you must vigorously define "always" (Daily? Weekly?), "does" (On purpose? Are they just dumb?) and "that" (What is it specifically?).

Frustration Game

The granddaddy of all games. One player's behavior frustrates another player. It's probably the most common game in improv, as well as in sketch comedy and sitcoms. Many people consider it the only game. But I hesitate to assign the word "game" solely to frustration scenes because what's going on in a player's head is so similar to how players play the other game scenes. These scenes need several things to be successful: a firm base in reality, a player with an absurd behavior, and a player frustrated by the absurd behavior. Let's look at each of these.

A firm base in reality simply means that the scene takes place in a recognizable location with recognizable people. This recognizable context, filled with recognizable human behaviors, allows for a contrast when an absurd point of view is expressed. An even slightly askew behavior will be visible when set against a glaring reality.

Can scenes take place in space or in a wizardly boarding school? Yes. Just know that the audience must see real human behaviors. When an audience hears "job interview," they know exactly what to expect from this situation in considerable detail. When they hear "flying broom class," they certainly make assumptions but are generally in the dark.

The absurd behavior does not need to be exceptionally absurd. It just needs to not fit into the reality presented. It doesn't have to be a reversal of expected behavior, or even a particularly clever take on behavior. A doctor afraid of blood or a kleptomaniac bank teller, while clever ideas, are no funnier than a stoner doctor or a talkative bank teller.

In fact, clever premises can be a bit of a trap, because they can make us feel that once we reveal the clever premise we've done all the work we need to do for a successful scene. In fact, our scene, and our workload, have only just begun at that point. Strong players don't need funny ideas; they make simple ideas funny by playing them well.

The last piece of the puzzle is the frustrated player: the straight man. This role is deceptively difficult, because while the rules for playing it are simple (react as you would in life), it asks us to do things (ask questions, say no, get angry) that go against the spirit of improv. The character must fight for what she wants while the actor knows she must lose. As the straight person, you represent the feelings of the audience. Faced with a talkative bank teller, they too would act the same way. You must not only ask questions, you must ask smart questions. You must work to figure out and understand the absurd person's point of view. Of course, you never will. That's why it's frustrating. You must allow yourself to be frustrated.

Please note that anger is not frustration, although they may look similar. Frustration carries along complex feelings like disappointment, failed expectations, and the notion that one's will is being resisted. These are valuable components to defining a point of view. Anger is simpler and more visceral and only implies the general notions of being hurt or denied something.

More Scenes Are Ruined by Unasked Questions Than by Asked Questions

Here's a scene that gets under my skin, not because it's stupid or unreal but because it's often poorly played. It's the "You know how you let me borrow your car last night? I'm not sure where it is now" scene.

The problem arises when car-owning player refuses to drop what they're doing and launch a thorough investigation to find their car. They just kinda get mad and wag a finger and go back to polishing the china.

If you've done improv before, you've probably been told to have a point of view and/or a physical activity (don't drop it!) and/or not to argue or ask questions. In real life, if someone started a conversation with "I can't find your car," unless you're giving someone CPR, you would stop what you're doing and find your car. "What?" "Where is it?" "Were you drunk?" "Are you still drunk?" "Retrace your steps. Where were you last night?" "No, it won't just turn up, put your shoes on and let's go find it." Again, audiences don't come to check your don't-ask-questions homework.

The frustrater must remember that his goal is not just to say funny things but also to frustrate. This opens doors to things other than doing his "thing" more. He can apologize sincerely or insincerely, he can resist accepting his behavior, accept his behavior begrudgingly, or accept it honestly and try to change, only to fail. The frustratee must remember that she may call out her partner for his absurd behavior and that– while the improviser may be trying to stay in the scene – her job is to behave as a real person would behave, which might mean leaving the scene if compelled to. As these scenes play out, it's important for the frusrater to not be too aggressive, lest he force his partner to leave. The frustratee must accept apologies and allow water to flow under the bridge (at least until they're both ready to end the scene!).

Assumption 5:

The audience does not know the rules of improv or your form and will not judge you based on them.

I've already mentioned a few things Chicago is known for. We can add world-class museums, thick pizza, and cold weather but I doubt those things are why you picked up this book. Chicago is also known for something that it has more of than any other city in the world. If you are into this something, then Chicago is your Mecca. I'm speaking, of course, about movable bridges. With more than sixty, Chicago has more drawbridges than any city in the world.

The Chicago River originates at Lake Michigan and travels west through downtown Chicago, slicing the city in half, north and south. After a mile the river splits into a north and south branch, further dividing the city east and west. This extensive waterway allowed the city to flourish. But it also created problems when people, barges, trains, cars, and ships needed to move around. The solution was movable bridges.

The bridges have many different designs. There is the vertical lift bridge, the single-span jackknife bridge, the rolling lift bridge, and the most common: the trunnion bascule bridge. Despite their design differences, these bridges all solve identical problems, since the river's width doesn't change much and there aren't any high bluffs or rocky outcrops to negotiate. A bunch of different bridges, all doing the same thing. For the boats, cars, trains, and people, the inner workings of the bridges are completely hidden, and as long as they get under or across, they couldn't care less. The designs all work.

Chicago also has more improv than any city in the world. Just like the bridges, the improv comes in many different designs. There is short form, long form, fast improv, slow improv, improv with twelve actors, improv with two actors, even improv with one actor. Which is best?

Despite being quite different from each other, they all solve the same problem: entertain an audience for 25 to 45 minutes. And while a particular design may not be implemented well, the designs themselves aren't flawed. (Just because a two-person show failed doesn't mean there's something wrong with all two-person improv.) Despite this, there is an attitude that there's a right way and a wrong way to play.

An audience member has never approached me after a show to tell me I was improvising incorrectly. (Though I have had some fellow performers apologize to me for breaking a rule after a funny scene.) Does the audience know that they're not supposed to laugh when a player commits a foul? Should the rules of improv be listed in the program? Of course not. The audience came to have fun, to laugh, and to relax. They just want to "use our bridge" and don't really care how it works. When we're onstage, their attention is on us. Why should our attention be on satisfying rules that the audience isn't aware of? Instead, since audiences do understand basic human interactions, we should follow the human moments as they arise and play them honestly.

Rather than playing to satisfy the rules, play the moment wherever it takes you.

Anything can happen.

Notes

I don't often yell at my students. In my experience, most players are sincerely trying to get it right, and their mistakes are honest. Very few make mean-spirited choices, so why harp on mistakes? As teachers and directors, we must be careful to give notes on a player's active choices and not on moments of confusion that they have little responsibility for. I'd also rather give a single, simple note concerning the moment a scene went awry and move on, as opposed to giving detailed notes on their failed attempts to right the sinking ship. Let's spend our time learning to be good sailors rather than good bailers.

With that in mind, here are some of the more common moments where things go awry. This is not a complete list, just a few common concerns that arise when I teach.

Move Tax

All choices are playable. There's not a fixed pile of mistake moves and another pile of correct moves.

Some choices, however, create a complicated reality or make the scene so unsavory that it's no fun to play. Typically, these choices are called mistakes. However, many of these mistakes can get huge laughs from an audience. (This apparent contradiction is explained by improv's dual nature as an art and a spectacle.) These funny mistakes are generally used on purpose by a player when a scene isn't going very well and the player become desperate for a laugh. Here are a few:

-Walking into a scene as a movie director and saying, "Cut!", as though the scene were taking place on the set of a movie the whole time but no one knew it.

-Playing the opposite of your natural impulse. After finding out Grandma is sick, a player might yell, "Hooray!"

-Turning a scene into an unsuccessful attempt at sexual roleplaying. "Take off the Obama mask, honey, this isn't working."

-Making your partner crazy. "Did you forget to take your meds this morning?"

In truth, you can make all those moves work, but you must pay the tax. The tax is that you must now live in the new reality your move has created. Players are very willing to turn a confusing scene into poor sexual roleplaying – it'll get a big laugh – but they aren't prepared to live in the sincere emotional space experienced by a couple that is having bedroom problems. It's funny that your crazy sister forgot to take her meds, but the reality of having to manage a person who's off her medication is not usually funny. Players will drop those lines and soak in the laugh but then quickly retreat from them.

"You gotta know the rules before you can break them." I've never liked that expression. If they're eventually going to be useless, you've probably picked the wrong rules in the first place. I prefer to say that some scenes are really easy to get into but really hard to get out of. What all the above moves have in common is that they'll probably get a laugh from the audience, and that makes them attractive to a player. What makes them unattractive to an experienced player is the high tax that comes with them. If there are high tax moves, there must also be low tax moves. Living the simple reality of a scene is a low tax move: "Grandma's dead, how terrible."

Navigating the "What Next?" Moment

Many scenes – scenes that are both played well and played poorly – have naturally occurring moments during which the characters don't have anything to say. This happens in life, too, perhaps during a natural pause or the moment after a topic has run its course. What next?

Some players get desperate and invent something weird or strange in an effort to reboot the scene, or they go back to the old topic over and over again. Move on. What would be a reasonable topic of conversation for these two people to talk about next? If the scene is about two jocks discussing the hotness of different cheerleaders, maybe they talk about squashing nerds next. Or about scoring some beers or porno mags. Take the simple route. Rather than playing what could be true, play what is probably true.

Playing Emotionally Bulletproof

You must allow yourself to be emotionally affected by your partner's words and actions. When someone deflects frustration or tries to stay above it, I say they're being emotionally bulletproof. It usually happens when someone tries to play high status or bored or uninterested. They get so caught up in playing the boss or stoner or bored housewife that they forget to react to what's going on in each moment of the scene.

Some actors decide that their character simply wouldn't emotionally react to anything, ever. This is a dangerous and difficult choice. While playing a drill sergeant may not provide you a wide range of emotions, you must emotionally acknowledge and "tip your hat" to the actions of your scene partner. A small scowl or a grunt will do. The stuffy Victorian father will not emote on principle, but a good actor will find ways to portray the fight going on inside as he shoves his emotions down upon learning that his daughter wants to marry the chimney sweep.

Not Leaving a Scene

Sometimes to maintain the integrity of a moment it is imperative that a player leave the scene. If the talkative bank teller simply refuses to process your deposit, you must demand to see the manager. If the teller informs you he is the manager (trying to win the moment) then you must leave. "Thank you for your time, but I'm leaving." You're not abandoning your partner; you're playing the reality of the moment and the audience will love you for it. When you leave, your savvy scene partner will relent, apologize, and agree to play nice (only to purposefully screw up later!). If your scene partner is over-playing their absurd behavior and/or trying to win, they'll let you leave, then turn to me and shrug, as if to say, "The scene was going great until he walked out; please give them a note." If you're the straight man, it isn't your job to stay in a scene; it's your partner's job to keep you there.

Always Playing Negative

When I give my students permission to say no and be uncool with what's going on, some do so in every scene from that day forward. Even in scenes when their partner initiates with a clear follow-me that asks them to play with, they magically find some way to play against. As a teacher or director, it's your job to call out the players who always take the negative role and force them to play with just as often. Many times playing negative goes hand in hand with being emotionally bulletproof; an actor who is uncomfortable with emoting can avoid doing so by taking angry "against" choices.

Obsessed With Getting It Right

I hate saying "Forget all the rules and just have fun," but some people could be helped by surgically removing all the improv advice they've ever been given. They think there's a secret formula, a recipe that will guarantee success. This shows up in their play when instead of being in the moment they're analyzing it. The point missed by the technique-obsessed is that all the advice and teaching in the world will never tell you what to improvise. Which leads to ...

Obsessed With the Way Others Play

Comedy nerds are actually comedy historians. It's great that you have discovered (and can tirelessly analyze) what others have created, but now it's time for you to create. Why did Monet choose to paint water lilies? Why did Shakespeare choose to write about Italian teenagers? Figure out what exists in the real world that you find deeply funny. The answer won't be in improv books or funny movies. It will be out in the world. (My own improv bloomed while temping in downtown Chicago.)

In the liner notes to Public Enemy's album *Apocalypse 91*, Chuck D says, "You rap about what you know." I say it this way: The fake lives you improvise are as rich and interesting as the real life you live. The best players play like they want to play. They've carved out a section of improv technique and it's their style. Discover your style.

(Although... If you're still in school, it's unreasonable to expect that you have a tremendous catalog of life experience to fall back on. Don't worry. You know a ton about what it means to be in school and the realities of how young people live and interact. Don't feel ashamed about improvising about that.)

Needing to Win and Playing Chess

Advice from the traditional theater world is often brought into improv. For instance: in a scene, it's important to have a strong motivation and an objective, and to work to overcome obstacles. It's not bad advice for playing a scene that has already been written, in which the character's fates are determined.

But in improv, where we don't know who will ultimately win and who will lose, it's pretty easy to create a situation in which neither player will relent. They both feel the need to work to win the scene in order to demonstrate their objective and strong motivations. As the players go back and forth, coming up with increasingly improbable and/or "witty" reasons to explain why they're right (I call this playing chess), the audience slowly loses interest. The solution here is the same as with any impasse: someone must lose without changing their character.

Being Funny

Please feel free to be funny. Just be careful to not step outside of the reality of the scene to do it. When someone breaks the moment for a joke, it strains the audience's perception of the reality. If the audience quits believing in the reality of your scene, they'll stop caring.

If your show is fast and loose with lots of short scenes, then any damage to the moment is mitigated by the fact that the scene will be over very soon. But if you're going for a longer scene and your scene partner breaks the moment for a joke, you might ask them, in character, "Are you trying to be funny right now?" Asking this question brings the scene back into a real world context.

Playing the Premise

Sure, that bread truck needs to get loaded. I understand that if mom gets home before the house is clean, she'll freak. But, ultimately, the completion or noncompletion of a task is not important. When players get stuck on creating obstacles and solutions to get a job done, they're missing the true scene, which is how the people feel about having to do the job and how they feel about having to do it with each other.

Melodrama Scenes

Melodrama is when we, the audience, are told how we should feel about a situation, usually via large emotional choices, rather than being given an honest scene with enough information for us to understand the characters' feelings. In general, melodramatic scenes happen when two reasonable points of view collide and neither is supported with enough detail to gain our empathy. This also happens when players confuse playing real with playing heavy situations, like someone having cancer or wanting a divorce. The actors feel like they're being vulnerable and really "going there," but, sadly, there's an emptiness behind their work. You must present your partner with a road map of information that lays out the path to explain your characters' feelings.

Accommodating

Also called being polite. It happens when one player makes excuses for another player's inappropriate behavior. It has the effect of eliminating the weird choice. If a player is trying to be weird by talking loudly and their partner either ignores it or explains it away

("I wish that truck never hit you that affected the part of your brain that controls vocal volume"), it undoes the choice. You aren't the other guy's scene partner, you're his sister or boss or parent or lover or bank teller, and you must behave appropriately. This could mean asking questions, saying no, laughing while saying no, accusing, or leaving.

3.

SHOW GAMES

The last section explored scene games. This section will tackle a concept called show games. The definition of a show game is tricky. It's easier to point at examples than it is to give a textbook definition. I'll try to do both, starting with an example.

Here's a problem that can only be solved with show game play. Let's pretend I get an improv troupe together and tell them to perform the movie *Ferris Bueller's Day Off* onstage. It must be word for word, the exact length of the movie, and the players may not use any sets, props, or costumes. It may not sound too difficult – there are many great scenes with hilarious dialogue that will be fun to play. What happens when you get to a scene with no dialogue? Specifically the scene where (spoiler alert!) two parking garage attendants take the Ferrari joyriding through Chicago? It's a memorable scene. We see the skyline, the car crest a hill, and a close-up on the attendants' faces. How do you present it? Remember: no sets, no props, no costumes. You do it with show games.

The bulk of a typical long form show is made

up of scenes. Everything else is a game. In that sense, the definition of a game is simply that it is not a scene. Scenes are defined as two or more characters engaged in dialogue that affects each person emotionally, is generally truthful, and presented without extreme affectation. Show games typically involve the full cast and, similar to scene games, may contain an outside-of-the-moment understanding or agenda between the players. The purpose is not to honestly portray the lives of the characters onstage but to create atmosphere and information and possibly make pointed comments about the suggestion or theme of the show. This could require big, over-the-top acting and affectation that would frowned upon in a scene.

Movies provide good analogies when trying to distinguish scenes from games. Imagine a scene in a movie where a woman is telling a man she no longer loves him. This is a scene. In the next moment, a helicopter is rescuing the man from a rooftop during a gunfight. In our improv language, this is a show game. Four high schoolers riding in a car talking about their first sexual experiences is a scene. Those same four high schoolers trying LSD while the other players portray a chaotic montage of talking fish, melting walls, and upset parents is a game. Action, quickened pace, and an absence of true dialogue are good indicators of a game.

Games can be used as simple connective bits between scenes or as complex recurring devices that open the show and provide a framework to directly explore themes. The most common use for this kind of game is to begin a show (called an opening) and within a show to provide a change of pace. Either way, their purpose is to inspire the improv scenes that follow them. The form called the Harold opens with a presentational, full-cast game that's used to inspire the entire show that follows. Some shows use monologues or imaginary locations created by the cast as inspiration for scenes.

To help you understand how games work, this section includes several simple games explained in full. My comments to the actors are in italics. While games are all improvised, there are common structures or templates that come up. This list of common structures is included to get people familiar with the rhythm and feel of games.

Please know that is not an exhaustive list, nor did Del Close keep a secret list of all possible games in a safe deposit box. Just like improv scenes, they are created in the moment, both in content and in structure. While there are an infinite number of games waiting to be discovered, notice what the few I have chosen to explain have in common: a simple set of rules the full cast agrees to and plays. To highlight the inspirational quality of group games, I'll also describe some scenes that could be inspired by each game.

There are also an infinite number of ways to play each game in this list. Here's a cooking analogy: béchamel sauce is one of the five mother sauces of French cooking. If you can make this simple white sauce, you can make a multitude of different sauces by swapping out a few ingredients. The cheese sauce in macaroni and cheese and the gravy on biscuits and gravy differ by only one or two ingredients. Consider the six games below as "mother sauce" games. With some experimentation and inspiration, you can use them to create an infinite number of unique games.

We See Eight

In We See Eight, the players take the stage together, but rather than playing different characters, each person plays the same character – like a full-cast general agreement game. By having the entire cast put on the same character, we're able to explore a point of view more deeply.

Could We See Seven or Nine?
You don't need eight actors to make this work. You can do it with more or fewer actors as well. We See Eight is a legacy name coined many years ago by someone in some group that no one remembers. I also like it because of the assonance. My examples will all involve eight people.

Here's how I'd explain We See Eight to a class:

Eight actors line up across the stage. I will say "We see eight blanks," and you must all become whatever it is I choose to fill the blank with. It could be high school nerds, nervous doctors, or overprotective mothers. Your characters are not in the same place — you are each in your own space and, as characters, cannot hear or react to what the others say. If you did, we'd have a scene and not a game. As actors, you can certainly hear what the other actors are saying. In fact, you're required to listen to the other players and make sure you're defining the character the same way and make each response explore more deeply than the previous one. You may speak in any order. Ready? We see eight overprotective mothers.

Actor 3 (Steps forward, delivering his line straight out to the audience): Don't cross the street without looking both ways. (After this line he steps back upstage.)

Actor 5 (Steps out and rather than looking at and addressing Actor 3's imaginary child, she speaks straight to the audience): Don't walk anywhere without looking both ways. (This actor also steps back after her line, starting a pattern of actors stepping forward, delivering their lines, and stepping back.)

Actor 1: Don't cross any streets.

Actor 7: A life of sin is not a life.

Actor 5: You have your mother. Do you need other friends?

As clear as the suggestion of overprotective mothers may seem, it actually has a bit of wiggle room. Overprotective mothers come in different flavors. There is the uber-religious, must-save-child-from-sin mother, and there's the possessive, we're-best-friends-forever mother. There is also the unreasonably cautious, danger-lurks-everywhere mother. The above example started out as unreasonably cautious, then veered into uber-religious and possessive mom territory. It is important that the players agree on which one they're all playing and play that mother exclusively. This game is an exploration of one point of view, and the more narrowly it's defined, the more deeply we can explore it. Could it change and evolve? Sure, but not four lines in.

You started out as unreasonably cautious mom. You are all that mom.

Actor 6: Don't forget your mittens and your hat.

Actor 8: Don't leave the house without wearing your thermal underwear.

Actor 2: Don't leave the house without your rape whistle.

Actor 4: Or your wilderness survival kit.

Repetition of verbal patterns like "Don't leave the house ..." is a good way to keep things tightly defined, but it's not required for success.

Actor 1: Take this emergency radio beacon.

Actor 5: You'll also need this signal mirror and Native American phrase book.

Actor 3: Here's a flare pistol.

Actor 7: And a real pistol. Be careful!

If this example had opened a show, a number of ideas could easily be turned into scenes, which is a principal purpose of games. From the notion of an urban child needing wilderness survival skills, an actor could start a scene by squatting with his ear to the ground and saying, "The copier on five is out of toner." The comment about crossing the street safely could inspire a scene starting with an actor arrogantly blowing a whistle and saying, "All right, kids, obey the crossing guard or pay the price!" While the word "worry" was never used explicitly, the concept of worrying runs through everything. In a worry-inspired scene an actor could nervously sway and stammer, "So, basically I'm not saying that I shouldn't have a raise, or that I couldn't do more to get one, just that ..."

None of these possible scenes I've suggested include an overprotective mother. Not that it would be wrong to have an overprotective mother scene, but we just spent several minutes exploring overprotective mothers, and it might be difficult to play an original overprotective mother scene that's more than just listing whatever was just said.

Zero, One, Infinity

How many overprotective mother scenes can we play following an opening game about overprotective mothers, as in the example above? I'm sure we're physically capable of doing a large number of them. The question is more about artistic choice. As the directors of our own show, how many overprotective mother scenes do we want to present to the audience?

As a rule of thumb, I suggest one of the following options: no scenes that use the suggestion literally, only one scene that uses the suggestion literally, or *all* scenes using the suggestion literally. As interesting as it is to get a variety of scenes inspired by but not including overprotective mothers, it's also impressive to have an entire run of different overprotective mother scenes.

During a show, We See Eight would begin with a player verbally initiating the We See Eight structure. Here's how I explained this next step:

Rather than me shouting "We see eight," any of you can shout it out. Anyone inspired by the last line about a mother giving a child a pistol?

Actor 8: We see eight incompetent cops.

Actor 5: You had to smash that car window because it's your car and you locked your keys in it? Okay, I'll buy that.

The overprotective mothers had you each stepping forward, saying your line, and then stepping back. Make this one look different.

> Actor 6 (steps forward and kneels, and stays knelt after his line): So you're hypoglycemic and needed to steal that candy bar? Okay, but just this once!

> Actor 2 (steps forward and stands behind Actor 6, almost like a family photo): You're taking this cocaine to the police station to turn it in? Sounds reasonable to me.

> Actor 7 (he and all subsequent actors play into the family photo staging): Yes, my car *is* dirty. It's very thoughtful of you to take it to the car wash.

Like overprotective mothers, there are many different flavors of incompetent cop. This flavor is "catches the criminal but is easily duped." Awesome. It's no better or worse than stupid evidence gathering cop ("I got peanut butter on the fingerprints") or oblivious cop ("Why does the police station phone keep ringing!?") They're all fine –   just pick one. Also realize that the picking process happens in the moment. Everyone may have a flavor of incompetent cop in mind when it's first said, but once the first person speaks, everyone must jump on board with that idea. You have to pay close attention. Notice the specific pattern, define, and refine.

Continue being bad cops, but rather than shouting out "We see eight blanks," when someone feels inspired, just begin doing a new character. Also define a new physicality to go along with it.

Actor 4: You promise this isn't a pyramid scheme that would bilk old people of their Social Security checks? ... Okay.

Actor 1: It was a suicide and you arrived just after they shot themselves? Well, you better put that gun down or someone will think you shot them.

Actor 7 (pacing nervously around the stage and continues pacing after her line): I'm not stealing this car. My friend lent it to me and then totally forgot she did.

The opposite point of view! A crook making up bad excuses. The players should pick up on this and support this new voice. Changing the physicality along with the character point of view will help communicate to your partners that you are making a change. The timing of when to stop matching and make a change can be difficult to explain. Perhaps a change is warranted after 5 or 6 people present their idea or after a particularly funny contribution. The important point is that choices are firmly matched until a firm change is made, which is itself matched until the next change.

Actor 3 (begins pacing, as do the other actors): The guy on the corner told me specifically this was not cocaine but pastry flour.

Actor 4: Technically, I shot him, but the bullet went through a robber, who has now run off, and then hit this man, who is my dear friend and not someone I was hired to kill.

Cool. We started with overprotective mothers and ended with criminals making bad excuses. The changes weren't forced, because the trail of inspiration is easy to follow. In a show or during a rehearsal, a We See Eight would may go much further than three points of view.

It's also tricky to pick this up as quickly as my example illustrates. A good tip to get the changes to really stick is to break the physical pattern along with the verbal pattern. You don't have to stand in a line, you don't have to say "We see eight" before every change. You don't have to strictly follow the word structure of the previous person, but it can help tie down and define a point of view. You do have to support the first idea said. You do have to physically adopt the character and attitude, not just stand neutrally saying funny stuff. You should avoid acknowledging the other players or letting your characters be affected by them; this is not a scene. Dialogue would get in the way of our deep-dive exploration.

Scene Painting

As improvisers, we are not just responsible for what the audience hears. We also are responsible for what they see. This game, scene painting, is about building environments by describing what can be seen in them. The closest analog to scene painting is found in movies, when a director slowly pans the camera across a room, leaving the viewer to pick out the details. Directors like Wes Anderson almost overwhelm the audience with the level of visual detail in their compositions. Again, there are many right ways to do this. I'll explain one way of doing this, as I would to a class.

One at a time you will take the stage and describe an object you see and where you see it. You may either introduce a new item or you may add something to a previous object. Once you have described your object, leave the stage. Don't worry about walking around other people's objects as you take the stage (which would create a spectacle game), but do carefully place your objects with respect to earlier objects. Listen to what objects are being created and have all objects point to one, clear context.

Actor 2 (upstage, center): There is a fire in a fireplace in the back of the room.

Actor 4: The fireplace has a large, dark wooden mantle over it.

Actor 8 (downstage from fireplace): A bearskin rug is in front of the fireplace.

Actor 1: To the right of the rug is a pair of black, high-heeled shoes.

Actor 5: To the left of the rug is a coffee table.

Actor 3: On the table are two Champagne glasses, nearly empty.

Actor 6: One has a deep, red lipstick stain on the rim.

Actor 8: The walls of the room are covered with very modern-looking abstract art.

Actor 7: To the left of the glasses, tossed carelessly across the table, is a black tuxedo jacket.

Actor 4: Continuing to the left, a slinky, sequined dress is thrown over the back of a chair.

Actor 2: To the left of that, on the floor, is a pair of men's black dress shoes partially covered by a pair of tuxedo pants.

Actor 1: There's a floor-to-ceiling window to the right of the fireplace.

Actor 3: We see a city skyline out of the window.

Actor 5: This room is at least 30 floors off the ground.

Actor 6: Beside the fireplace is an open door.

Actor 3: Inside the door we see the corner of a bed.

Actor 7: A man's foot hangs off the bed, toes down.

Actor 5: Blood drips from the man's toe.

Actor 8: In the back of the room, through another open door, we see the frosted glass pane of a shower enclosure.

Actor 1: Through the frosted glass we see the silhouette of a woman.

Not one word has been spoken by a character, but a story has been told. This happens in movies all the time. Pictures are used to convey a message or set a tone. This example is quite cinematic, but know that scene painting is about using pictures to tell a story and not about listing movie clichés. It requires the players to listen to each other and drive toward a common image. If you aren't listening, duplicate objects or objects that negate each other may be created.

A long form could use the environment painted as a location for scenes to take place in. Or the scene paint could be used as a way of generating ideas for scenes, even though no scenes explicitly take place in the painted environment. The above example includes the ideas of dates, formal attire, showers, and bear rugs, among other things. Each could be used to create a scene that in no way looks like the scene paint. Taking a large, complex mass of information and breaking it down into component parts is called deconstruction.

Another option might be to paint three scenes in rapid succession and have them appear as locations for scenes randomly throughout the show. A form could use a quick free-for-all scene paint with silly objects done with a smile, or a form might require a calmer and more tense mood, asking the players to be disciplined and careful. Could actors stay onstage and portray the objects with their bodies? Sure.

Character Painting

To carry forward the béchamel sauce analogy, character painting could be thought of as a variation on scene painting. Its conceit is that actors can portray characters that appear in the scene painting, and then be painted themselves. Let's go back to the example of the (probably) murderous woman created in the above scene painting.

Actor 8: In the back of the room, through another open door, we see the frosted glass pane of a shower enclosure.

Actor 1: In the frosted glass, we see the silhouette of a woman.

Someone take the stage and be the woman in the shower. The rest of you may continue painting the environment. You may also paint her.

Actor 5 takes the stage and begins to pantomime that she is showering.

Actor 3: This woman has long, jet-black hair.

Actor 4: She appears to be in her mid-30's.

Actor 6: Steam from the shower partially obscures her face.

Actor 7: She has a tattoo on her foot of a dragon eating its tail.

Showering woman, you may leave the shower. Do whatever you like, but you must remain silent. The other actors will describe your actions.

Actor 5, portraying the woman, leaves the shower, puts on a robe and pantomimes pulling something out from under the bed.

Actor 1: She pulls a metal briefcase out from under the bed.

Actor 3: She does not know the combination to open the lock.

Actor 6: Her robe is white terry cloth, monogrammed with a DKH.

Actor 4: Those are not her initials.

Good fun! Could this character be in our show? Could this room be in our show? Could the show explore what happened leading up to this event? Or what happens next? The answer to all of those questions is yes.

Before you rush off to do that, here's another question with a yes for an answer. Could we do a show with none of these people or places? Yes. Narratives can be hard to improvise. Don't feel that just because you reference people or places from the beginning of the show that an audience will immediately forgive bad scene work. In fact, forcing players to directly use plot and character points from any opening device loads them up with obligations before they even step onstage. It's easier to simply let the themes and images affect our scenes subtextually.

A quick deconstruction of the scene paint reveals themes of wealth, romance, sex, murder, black widows. Those and many others could inspire scenes that, as far as plot goes, have nothing to do with the story laid out in the scene paint. They would be in no way incorrect. Could we revisit this story with scene painting later in our show (a reset, discussed in the next chapter)? By all means. Perhaps our reset scene paint is of the inside of a police detective's office, and not until the very end does someone put a "missing" poster on a bulletin board.

Character painting can also be done by itself, independent of scene painting. Three actors can take the stage and are painted either in order or all at once. Through the painting we might learn, for example, how they know each other. The painted actors could take turns adding bits of in-character monologue between the paints.

Narrated Story

The character paint example highlights an interesting concept. The actor playing the mysterious woman chose to look under the bed, but it was the other actors, the scene painters, who defined what she was grabbing. One actor is pantomiming actions while the others are describing actions. Who is leading and who is following? In true improv fashion, everyone is leading and everyone is following. This concept of silent actors providing action while outside voices provide narration is called the narrated story.

When teaching this to a class, I start with an old short form standard, the conducted story, only without a conductor. A group of people must tell a story together but only one person may speak at a time. No going in a set order, no pointing or other tricks to signify who speaks next. When someone feels like talking, they begin speaking. Typically improvisers are respectful, which is usually a good thing, but with this they may need to be encouraged to be "rude" and cut in before the current speaker has finished her sentence. By finishing each other's thoughts, they produce a story that is of the moment.

Once the group has gotten comfortable with that, I introduce this element: If you aren't speaking, you're acting out the story that's being told. You may be people, you may use your body to make objects or create the background, or you may use your mouth to make noises, but you must continue sharing the job of narration. Everyone is always doing something. Once someone has portrayed a particular character, can someone take that character over? Sure. Can the characters ever speak not as narrators but in their own voices? Go for it, but remember that this is a game and not a scene.

Monologues

Monologues come in two principal flavors: truthful monologues, in which an actor tells a story as himself, and character monologues, in which a character tells a story that's true to the character but made up by the actor.

Truthful monologues are just that: true stories told by the actor. They can be funny or touching or curious. Whatever type of monologue is done, it must contain plenty of details. And then more details.

The assumption is often that monologue should be funny, "There was this one time"-type stories, but monologues can also be a chance for the monologist to express his feelings or thoughts about a particular topic. In this case, rather than concentrating on the details of a story, the monologist presents detailed evidence to support his belief. The opinion that all bosses are evil may seem trite, that's fine as long as we get personal evidence that backs up that belief. "I'm basing this theory entirely on the behavior of the four bosses I've had. Boss number one forbade me from checking email or phone messages because he figured that since he didn't have a cell phone or the Internet when he was my age, I shouldn't need them either."

The thing to remember about truthful monologues is they must be true. The teller must trust that his story has value simply because it's true. No embellishments or "Sorry this is so boring" apologies. Fill it with details, don't apologize, and don't be afraid to open yourself up emotionally.

Character monologues are made-up stories in a character's voice. Sometimes they're half of a conversation:

Dina: Yeah, sorry. I ain't got the parts ... You could take it but I'd have to put it back together first ... Hey, we're all busy, right?

or told as a story from the character:

Dina: So I told the guy, I said I ain't got the parts. He says then he needs to take it and I'm like, sure, but it's in pieces on the floor. Then he starts doing the whole I'm-a-busy-man song and dance, like his time is more important than mine.

They may also have a context attached to them, like a dating service video or a *Survivor*-esque direct-to-camera interview.

Monologues can be used as show openers or in the middle as reset mechanisms (more on that in the next section.) A long-running show in Chicago called The Armando Diaz Experience features one cast member as a monologist opening the show with a truthful monologue and returning throughout to give more monologues. Many theaters use this format for shows, sometimes with local celebrities or people with interesting jobs or backgrounds providing the monologues.

Another show form, the Living Room, has the full cast discussing topics together, truthfully, as though they're all casually hanging out somewhere. This multi-person monologue concept can be used with any number of actors and can consist of either truthful or character monologues. A rule of thumb with monologues is that a single segment can consist of one long monologue, three medium-length monologues, or each cast member giving a two-to-three-sentence monologue.

Monologues have value beyond simply being

funny stories to inspire scenes; they can also set a mood. A series of quick monologues can set the pace of the show. While monologues may be entertaining as stand-alone stories, their function at the opening of a show is typically to inspire the scenes that follow them. The scenes inspired by the monologues do not have to be a retelling of the story. In fact, replaying the monologue is often discouraged. As with the games I've discussed, players listen to the story, deconstruct it, and perform scenes inspired by the pieces.

Putting Your Inspiration Into a Usable Form

Imagine a monologue that touches on themes of loss, disobeying authority, and laziness. (What a story!) No one of those themes is any more correct than the others, but for an improviser, some are easier to play and some may need some massaging before they're ready for the stage.

Imagine this: You're at an audition and you want to do your best work. Before your big scene, I give you a suggestion and you must use it onstage. Would you rather me say, "Your suggestion is loss. Go!" or "Your suggestion is lazy. Go!" I'm betting most people would want to hear "lazy." Why? As a description of behavior, it's easy for us to bring it into immediate action (or, in the case of laziness, inaction). It's a strong, clearly-defined point of view. Loss is ambiguous, and while it may imply sadness over a loss, it could also imply confusion at being lost. To complicate things further, sad and confused aren't behaviors but emotions felt by all people, regardless of point of view. A player might think she's playing a strong choice of sadness or confusion but never figure out who it is that's sad or confused.

The Behavior/Context exercise is a good example of working with easily digestible inspiration. The suggestions are clear behaviors and students rarely feel flat-footed in that exercise.

If you're struck by a theme like loss as your inspiration, great! Don't discard it. Just realize that you may need to massage it to make it ready for the stage. Namely, you need to turn it into an actionable behavior. You could play someone who's constantly sad and mopey, someone who's scatterbrained (lost), or perhaps a maudlin, nostalgic person always remembering past happiness. All of those choices are easier to play than "loss."

The Press Conference

The press conference is essentially a group frustration scene game. It requires good critical listening and patience. As an example, imagine a press conference given by a representative of the Nike shoe company addressing members of the media about its newest athletic shoe.

> Host: Ladies and gentlemen of the media, we at Nike are pleased to announce the release of our newest air-cushion-sole shoe ...
>
> (A hand is raised in the audience.)
>
> Host: A question?
>
> Reporter #1: Yes. You mentioned the shoe has a soul. So when it dies will it go to heaven?
>
> Host: Um ... no?

Reporter #2: What if my shoe has an evil soul? Will I go around kicking people?

Host: I'm afraid you've misunderstood me ...

Reporter #3: Where do you get all of the souls for your shoes? Aborted fetuses?

Host: No! You don't understand. When I said air-cushion sole I was referring to the bottom of the shoe, the sole, which is different from the soul or spirit that lives in us.

Reporter #4: I see, not s-o-u-l soul but s-o-l-e sole. So these shoes have no souls. So these are zombie shoes forever damned to walk the earth, never finding peace?

Host: No!

I'll stop it there but it could go on much longer. Let's break down that example. This scene really just has two characters: the presenter, who is reasonable, and the media members, who are unreasonable. It is played essentially like the frustration game variety of scene game. Each role has a specific job. Let's look at the media first.

The ultimate job of the media in this scene is to frustrate the presenter. What makes the above example frustrating is that despite the presenter's best efforts, the media still misunderstand everything told to them. Importantly, they all misunderstand it in the same way. While the questions are certainly stupid, they're not random. They push the core misunderstanding (soul vs. sole) as far as possible. There is a simple trick to making this work; coincidentally, it's the same trick used in every other game: Listen to and respect the first thing said. In this case, whoever asks the first question will set the tone for the press conference.

In the above example, the first question confused sole and soul. What if the first question was this: "You said there is air in the shoes? Like the Hindenburg? Are my shoes going to explode?" If that's the first question, the second question shouldn't be about shoes having evil souls; it should instead push the idea that these air-filled shoes are prone to catastrophic explosions. "Maybe you could use helium in the shoes. It won't explode and would let the people wearing them jump really high." Each question builds on the last, pushing one central conceit. The person who asks the first question is the drummer for the band. Everyone else must play to that beat.

You only have to play this game once to realize it can be crushingly funny and fun to do – but remember, your job is to frustrate the host, not just rattle off funny things for the audience. Most of the time those two goals converge, but every now and again, they diverge. You may have a very funny line, but if you aren't listening to the other questions, the moment into which it could fit might have already passed.

In the above example, the final question acknowledges the presenter and even concedes some points before pushing the confusion further on a slightly altered course. It's more frustrating for the presenter to have people say they're listening (even repeating back to her what she just said) only to confuse the issue even more than it is to just be barraged by random questions.

If the job of the media is to frustrate, it's the job of the presenter to get frustrated. Earlier I said this game plays like a group frustration scene game. Its scenic nature is evident here. The presenter must be affected: no emotionally bulletproof improv play.

Frustration is different than anger. It starts as confusion and builds and grows to anger, but it is never evil or vindictive. It carries the implication that expectations aren't being met. "This really isn't that difficult. Why are you having problems?" Also, for this game to work, the presenter can't just shoot down stupid questions – "Nope," "Dumb," "Really? Next!" She has to let the blows land. We have to see the presenter struggle to understand the questions. Before someone can lose patience, they must first be patient.

The presenter can never cross the line into the absurd, or the game is over. In the above example, if the presenter were to say, "We get the souls from Chinese political prisoners," guess what? The seemingly absurd media has now been out-absurded. (But they could then launch into reasonable questions at this point and we'd get a good reverse press conference game!) The game relies on frustration, and any moves to mitigate or ease the frustration release the tension. In the above example, the presenter's topic and brief presentation are very dry and reasonable, something you might see at an official corporate event. That's the point. Absurdity needs a reality to play off of. It's the job of the presenter to provide that reasonable point of view.

This game can get pretty wild: watch out for people talking over each other. The media shouldn't be allowed to steamroll the presenter. They need to find a balance. Again, the ultimate goal is to frustrate, not to get into some kind of joke sprint. You may also find that the occasional off-topic question gets a huge laugh. Sure, it can be quite funny, but it's because it's out of place that it's funny. If everyone asks off-topic questions, they're no longer out of place. Off-topic questions are an accent, like the olive in a martini: only one will do. No one orders a ten-dollar glass of olives.

What makes the press conference fit into the béchamel sauce analogy so nicely is that the context (press conference) can be easily swapped out with another with no effect on the rules (e.g., follow the first question). How different is a press conference from a museum tour with a reasonable tour guide and stupid museumgoers? Or story time with Grandma? Or a "Sales staff, get in here" business meeting?

The press conference is essentially a group frustration scene with two points of view. Many group scenes are press conferences in disguise, and many large cast scenes slide into a press conference without the initiator intending them to. I sometimes use the press conference as an exercise in listening. It's also good for teaching patience and the ability to observe and serve the whole of a group scene.

When used to begin a show, the press conference does a good job of exploring the suggestion. In the example, a suggestion of shoes has opened up the topics of heaven and hell, violence and bullying, abortion, and zombies. Any scenes inspired by these topics are now fair game. Note that the press conference has some scenic elements that might run contrary to the aesthetic style you hope to achieve at the top of your show. As a game or reset within the show, however, the press conference (or a game based on the press conference structure) is a great way to bump the energy.

Movie Trailer

Using the six games discussed as a starting point, and with some experimentation, you can create – a la béchamel sauce – thousands of unique games. If you're really sharp, you can create them in the moment onstage. Many theater warmups and games like those used by Viola Spolin can also be brought over into the world of long form games. While they may not be ready-made for the stage, mirror exercises, organic machines, rituals, and word pattern games are fertile ground for creating new games, particularly more abstract, movement-based games.

Here's a fun compound game that combines elements of other games. It's called the movie trailer. The objective is to improvise a movie trailer. Sounds easy, but remember that you have no sets, props, or costumes.

Here are some soft rules to keep things moving forward. There are only three roles the players can play, and while they can switch off and share the roles, they can only be one of the three things at any given time. Those roles are the narrator ("In a world where danger is served hot, one man ..."), the scene painter ("We see the inside of a large science lab; it looks like NASA mission control, with computers and people in white shirts and a large, light-up image of a volcano on the wall ..."), and actor ("Slow down, Professor. You want me to go into that volcano?!"). The narrator is offstage, the scene painter runs on to paint or show a close-up, and the actor stays onstage and acts.

Avoid switching roles midstream: "In a world, one man, dressed in a spacesuit, talks to this professor guy. Danger lurks in the underground science lab, and he says 'You're crazy.'" Did the narrator say all those things? The roles got jumbled and confused.

Something to pay attention to is how the actors firmly change locations without bringing characters forward. Movie trailers sometimes jump to something new without explaining it first. It may appear random at first but it will make sense.

Actor 1 (narrator): In a world where danger is served hot!

Actor 2 (scene painter): We see an overhead shot looking into the mouth of a volcano.

Actors 3 and 4 (actors): (They link hands and form a circle tipped toward the audience: this is the overhead shot.)

Actor 5 (actor): (He makes gurgling sounds in the middle of the circle.)

Actor 6 (narrator): One man has the power to keep his cool.

Actor 7 (scene painter): Cut to the skyline of New York City.

Actors 1, 2, and 3 (actors): (They portray tall buildings.)

Actor 4 (scene painter): We see a street view, morning rush hour.

All actors (actors): (They bustle around like business people.)

Actor 5 (scene painter): We see one man standing among the crowd.

Actor 6 (actor): (He stands calmly in the middle of the commotion.)

Actor 7 (scene painter): Slow motion! (Everyone moves in slow motion.)

Actor 1 (scene painter): Closeup on man.

(Everyone except Actor 6 leaves the stage.)

Actor 2 (narrator): His name is Roc Godbold.

Actor 3 (scene painter): He's wearing a skull earring. (Uses his hands to frame Actor 6's ear.)

Actor 5 (scene painter): Close-up on a teardrop tattoo on the corner of his mouth. (Uses hand to frame corner of mouth.)

Actor 6 (scene painter): Close-up on belt buckle. It is a cobra and a U.S. flag.

Actor 7 (scene painter): Cut to a science lab.

(Actor 6 and the scene painters leave the stage.)

Actor 1 (scene painter): Busy, NASA-mission-control-type lab with many technicians and computer bays. (The other actors take the stage as busy technicians.)

Actor 2 (scene painter): A caption on the bottom reads: "12 miles under the Pentagon."

Actor 3 (narrator): It's a race against time that no one wants to win.

Actor 5 (Scene painter): Roc Godbold enters with an egghead scientist.

(Actor 4 and Actor 6 enter as Godbold and scientist.)

Actor 7 (scene painter): The scientist clutches papers that spill out whenever he walks.

Actor 6 (actor): Mr. Godbold –

Actor 4 (actor): Call me Roc.

Actor 6 (actor): Certainly. It's Mount St. Satan. It's due for an eruption.

Actor 1 (scene painter): Behind them on the wall is a giant volcano diagram with lights and blinky things.

Actor 4 (actor): Find yourself a new hero, Doc. You know I can't do volcanoes. Not after what happened to Gloria.

Actor 2 (scene painter): Close-up on Godbold's eye as he stares off in the distance.

(Actor 2 uses his hands to frame Actor 4's eye.)

Actor 3 (scene painter): This image slowly cross fades and is replaced with a jungle landscape.

(Actor 4 leaves the stage.)

Actor 5 (scene painter): We hear the 'whomp-whomp' sound of a helicopter.

Actor 6 (scene painter): We hear the opening lick of "Fortunate Son" by CCR!

Actor 7 (scene painter): Our view is as if we're riding in the back of an army jeep. We see the backs of two people in the front seats.

(Actor 1 and 2 sit facing away from the audience.)

Actor 1 (actor, turns to look at the audience): This job is a real layup, no wet work.

Actor 4 (scene painter): The jeep's driver is wearing green army fatigues. The passenger is wearing khaki pants, a blue polo shirt, and a tan photographer vest with all the pockets.

Actor 3 (narrator): Some wounds never heal. And those that do don't always heal correctly or to as full an extent as we would like.

Not all movie trailers describe the entire movie. Some are just images. Many have strange cuts to unexpected places that only make sense later. Some have no character dialogue at all. Not all narrators are the "in a world" type. The audience is always the camera's perspective, so use that limitation as a challenge. Explore, have fun.

4.

SHOWS

Let's put a show together! In this section, I'll describe some simple show forms you can customize, and I'll give some examples of old forms. The old forms are not included for you to feel you must perform – they're included to inspire you to create on your own. Scenes and games comprise 98 percent of your show's content. The last 2 percent is the bits and pieces needed to hold the show together. Which bits and pieces you choose (and how you use them) go a long way toward determining the pace and tone of your show. Let's start with those bits and pieces.

Editing Scenes

Since long form shows lack an external director, the decisions about when scenes are over and what should come next are made in the moment by the players. This is called editing. Editing means deciding not just when a scene is over but what technique is used to signify the edit.

Consider movies. The ends of scenes are signaled by a blackout, a slow fade, or by simply cutting to the next scene in progress. By utilizing different editing techniques, a movie editor can create pace or suggest a mood. A horror movie is edited very differently than a rom-com.

The easiest place to edit an improv scene is when the audience laughs at it. That's a very simple way of looking at it. (Too simple, in fact.) Decisions about the show's pace and style can be expressed with the timing and techniques used for editing. Sometimes a scene may intentionally be held past a good laugh. Perhaps the players have decided their show will be made up of a small number of longer scenes played in a relationship style rather than a game style.

The two most common types of edits are the sweep edit and the tag edit.

Pace

When I was a young player, I wanted to play fast. As fast as I could. Tag-outs, character dashes, and cut-tos: I couldn't get enough. I didn't like slow scenes until I saw slow scenes played well. A show called Trio showed me that slow-paced or real scenes aren't about speaking slowly or making the characters have cancer. Playing slow doesn't mean improvising slowly; it means playing without jumping to conclusions until things are ready to happen.

A good way to define pace is to consider the ratio of scene time to real time. A fast-paced series of scenes and tag-outs will, in two minutes, transport the characters through hours, days, or years. A slow-paced scene will, in two minutes, transport the characters through two minutes of time. When scene time is compressed and much more stuff happens (or is implied to be happening) than could happen in real time, you're playing fast-paced. When scene time passes as real time would, you're playing slowly.

Here's an example of fast pace:

Stacy (bending as if to look in a car window, a little scared and hesitant): Oh man, sorry. I ran the heck out of that red light. You okay?
Ralph (sitting, dazed but calm): Ugh ... you hit me.

Stacy: Yeah, I, ummm. It wasn't that I was texting, per se ...

Herbert (makes a siren noise, enters with thumbs in belt): I'm a police officer. You ran the hell out of that light! You texting?

Stacy: Technically, I was braking when I entered the intersection ...

Herbert (grabs Stacy): Let's go!

Stacy: I wasn't texting!

Dick (offstage): Cut to jail!

Carlos (enters, waves off Herbert and Ralph, and sits on the corner of a chair and begins doing biceps curls): What you in for?

Stacy: I hit a guy with my car, but here's the thing ...

Carlos: Were you texting?

Cindy (enters, waves off Carlos, brings in the Ralph and has him sit, then sits on back of a chair with feet on the seat and pantomimes a gavel): Order, order in the court! Do you know why you are here?

Stacy: Your honor, I hit a man with my car. I was texting but my wife had just given birth ...

Cindy (isn't paying attention): ...

Stacy: Your honor?
Cindy: Sorry, I was umm ... ahhhh ...

Herbert (enters scene as cop): Were you texting?!?

Cindy: Not really ...

Carlos (waves off Herbert and Stacy, sits in a chair doing biceps curls, speaks to Cindy): What you in for?

That's fast pace. Forty-five seconds of scene time were used exploring what would probably take weeks or months of real time. This scene is full of game energy. The players are less interested in inhabiting characters than they are interested in driving them in and out of comedic situations.
Here's slow pace:

Stacy (bending as if to look in a car window, a little scared and hesitant): Oh man, Sorry. I ran the heck out of that red light. You okay?

Richard (sitting, dazed but calm): Ugh ... you hit me, man.

Stacy: Yeah, I umm. It wasn't that I was texting, per se ...

Richard: I saw you, you were texting.

Stacy: Wow, you are observant.

Richard: Was it important?

Stacy: What? Oh. OH! Yes! Very important. My wife is ... in labor.

Richard: Why are you still here?

Stacy: It literally just started. Contractions are like a four. On a one-to-ten scale. She was like, FYI, you may want to start making your way to the hospital, no rush.

Richard: No rush? You blew through that light!

Stacy: I was texting!

That is slow. Or slower. It takes minutes for the cops and the ambulance to arrive. Do we play out that time or compress it with a tag-out? Compress it by what degree? That is pace. The definition is academic. Being able to vary pace as a player is important. Being able to respect the pace of others (and not run on and tag out regardless of what's happening in the scene) is also important.

Sweep Edit

A sweep edit is performed by a player walking briskly in front of the action from one side of the stage to the other, "sweeping" it away. When a scene is swept, it's over and a new one begins. The actors onstage need to be aware that they have been swept and leave the stage. Generally the sweeper starts the next scene, but your group will decide what house rules they want to play with. It's considered bad form to sweep edit yourself from inside a scene. No one will arrest you for doing it, but it may engender ill will from the players who now have to run onstage and fill the void you created.

> (Samantha and Rick are sitting facing each other laughing.)
>
> Samantha: And I said, "That's my lemon!"
>
> Rick: Nice story, Grandma. Hey, look at the time.
> Harriet (from offstage, runs in front of Sam and Rick. They immediately drop character and leave the stage. Harriet takes center stage and speaks.): I just bought this scone and when I started ...
>
> (Ed sees that Harriet has started a new scene and runs onstage to join her. He thinks she's probably at a coffee shop (one was mentioned in the opening) so he takes the stage assuming he is a barista)
>
> Harriet: ... eating it I found a big hunk of ice in the middle.
>
> Ed: Did you keep your receipt? No? Hmmm...

Tag Edit

If a player wishes to start another scene but retain one or more of the onstage characters they may perform a tag edit. A player from the side steps into the scene and taps one of the players on the shoulder, tagging them out, which tells them to leave the stage. The untagged actors remain playing the same characters they played in the previous scene.

Here's an example of how a tag edit could work in an already existing scene.

> (Bernie and Diane are sitting side by side, as if in a car)
>
> Bernie (playing it cool): I thought that movie was pretty funny. Not as funny as you when you're tutoring me about English and stuff. You wanna go back to my place?
>
> Diane (emotionally tired): No, Bernie, I don't.
>
> Bernie: I didn't mean it like that. It's just that I thought you might like to look at my books or something.
>
> Gordon (enters, taps Diane on the shoulder. She quickly leaves the stage without saying anything. Gordon begins pantomiming playing darts and drinking a beer.)
>
> Gordon: Dude. Date with the luscious Diane. Tell me you got some!
>
> Bernie (nervous; as the same character, because he was not tagged out): Um ... Totally!
>
> (They high five and pound their drinks)

Through the use of a tag edit, the action has been pushed forward in time to some point after the date, when Bernie's buddy is asking for the play-by-play. The player who is tagged out should not get comfortable on the side of the stage. The person tagging in may not have a long scene in mind and the original player may need to tag back in.

Gordon: Gimme some details!

Bernie: I picked her up at –

Gordon: You can skimp on those details. What happened once you got her home?

Diane (enters and tags out Gordon, leaving Bernie. She stands, arms crossed, completely bored.): So you wanted to show me your books?

Bernie (nervous): Yeah. I said that. Over here.

Diane: I'm not going into your bedroom.
Bernie: It's just–

Diane: Ever.

Bernie: Since Coach made you start tutoring me I went from hating school and hating being tutored to hating school but liking being tutored.

Diane: Bernie, you're an idiot. And please don't refer to my father as "Coach" in front of me. "Coach" is the only honorific title that can be achieved without having any honor.

Bernie: Huh?

Diane has tagged in and thrown the action back to the date. Somehow Bernie has convinced her to come up to his place. Could Gordon tag back in and pull the action back to the bar? Sure. Could Gordon and Diane take turns tagging in, from bar to date and back, advancing the action until we learn about the date and Bernie's lies about the date? Totally. A series of tags that intentionally leave the same character onstage is called a character dash. When designing your own forms, or when doing organic Harold openings, a character dash is a cool technique to either introduce a character to the audience that they may meet later, or to use that character to explore themes.

Here's an example of how this character dash could continue, with more added characters:

Gordon (tags out Diane, taking the action back to the bar.): Third base, really? Dude! High five!

Gary (tags out Gordon. He stands up tall and barks his lines): Bernie, get in here! The rest of you hit the showers. I heard from Gordon that you got to third base with my daughter.

Bernie: You're not happy about it?

Gary: I'm furious!!!

Diane (tags out Gary): You told my dad that we got to third base?!?

Bernie: No! I told Gordon we got to third base.

When tags and sweep edits quickly follow one another in quick succession, it is called a run. Running in improv can be a fun way to elevate the pace of a show. Some teams will save a run for the end of their show (this is often referred to as a run-out or running out the show) in which they toss in every lost idea or loose thread in quick succession. An intra-show run can be a good way to inject energy and get a team on the same page.

> **Don't Worry About This Situation That Rarely Happens**
> I have known groups that shout "Freeze!" and/or clap to stop the action before they sweep or tag edit. The concern they feel is that if they don't freeze the scene immediately it will continue past a particular moment, making their idea invalid. Sure, that could happen, but as you get better you'll find that the disruption of the flow caused by stopping and restarting the action is more detrimental than the possibility of missing your moment. Sometimes experienced groups don't even tag: as a player enters the stage, they'll wave off the players they don't need with a quick, simple gesture.

Walk-ons

A player may also join the action onstage. This is called a walk-on. Some walk-ons are short, only consisting of a line or two. Other walk-ons may join the scene to stay. Some actors get into the habit of walking on to every scene. This is usually caused by uncontainable enthusiasm but can also be the result of a player with a controlling personality. An old improv adage is that the urge to walk on should be understood as the urge to edit, meaning that if you feel that a scene needs help perhaps the best way to help it is to cut it. It's not uncommon for groups to have soft rules about when players can or can't walk on (e.g., no walk-ons during the first third of a show).

Split Scenes

A split scene involves two scenes existing onstage at the same time, typically with one at stage left and one at stage right. The focus shifts between the two scenes. By keeping all the actors onstage, the transitions can be made more quickly and smoothly.

Here is an example of what the start of a split scene might look like:

> (Grace and Jen are sitting in chairs next to each other, pantomiming writing at desks.)
>
> Grace (whispering): Jen, this test doesn't make any sense.
>
> Jen (also quiet): I've already counted like five spelling errors. Is that part of the test?
>
> Norman (enters and stands just onstage right bringing with him another player, Dennis. He does not cross in front of or wave off Grace and Jen.): Another bourbon, Professor Williams?

Norman hopes to start a split scene demonstrating why the test the girls are taking is so confusing. The women recognize this, stay onstage, and stop talking but continue to pantomime their actions. They will speak again when they are inspired to speak, taking the focus from Norman and Professor Williams. When Norman or the professor feel like speaking they will do so, and the focus will naturally return to them.

> Dennis (drunk): I've been drinking bourbon?
>
> Norman: Since 4:30, sir.

Grace: Have you gotten to question six? It just says, "Sharon!!!!"

Jen: I think that's his ex-wife's name.

Grace: Then I guess it makes sense.

Dennis: Sharon!!!

Norman: Perhaps we should switch to coffee.

Dennis: Normy, you know I'm supposed to be writing a test right now. It's on European socialism. I'm not European, I don't plan on being European ... (barf!)!!

Jen: Does your test have a strange red stain on it?

Grace: No.

Jen: Gross.

Cut-to

When a scene implies that an event has happened or is about to happen, the players may want to move backward or forward in time to show that moment. A cut-to is similar to a movie flashback, but it could also be a flash-forward. It's accomplished by an offstage actor shouting "Cut to _____!" from offstage. The onstage actors are now playing in this new time/location. Just as with tags, the scene being cut to could be very short. Actors can yell "Cut back!" to return the action to the original scene.

Here's an example of how a cut-to could work:

(Carl and Liz are walking together.)

Carl: Explain to me why you thought it would be a good idea to take this shortcut through a dark alley.

Liz: If you want to beat the holiday shopping crowds you've got to be willing to think outside the box.

Carl: Outside the box? That's what you said when we trekked through two miles of Costa Rican jungle to avoid paying for a taxi to the resort.

Jim (offstage): Cut to the Costa Rican Jungle!

Carl (pantomiming lugging heavy bags, wiping his brow): This is supposed to be a vacation. Is this worth the ten pesos we're saving?

Liz (pantomiming hacking through jungle): Ask me again when you've got that cool, ten-peso piña colada in your hand.

Jim (offstage): Cut back!

Carl (back to walking through city): It was an all-inclusive resort. The drinks were free!

Liz: The experience? Priceless.

Play It, Don't Say It

Having an offstage actor yelling changes into a scene is bit extreme and, depending on your artistic sensibilities, may be too rough. It can also be abused by a lazy or controlling offstage player. Many times the same effect can be accomplished with a clever tag-out, especially if only one of the onstage actors is involved in the cut-to. If the cut-to puts both actors in a restaurant or business, a tagging-in actor could be a maître d' or a receptionist. They could also avoid literally tagging by making a forceful entrance and dropping a clear follow-me line to pull the actors into the time and place they wish to create. This move is more elegant than an offstage shout.

Soft Edits

The majority of sweep edits are executed after a line is said that elicits a big laugh from the audience. Like a stagehand in black entering a play to move a piece of the set, it may seem inelegant to have a player run across the stage to stop and start a new scene. That moment of awkwardness is generally covered by the audience's laughter. (The edit actually gives the audience a chance to laugh out loud without fear of missing anything – something they appreciate.)

It is not a rule, however, that edits must occur on a big laugh. If that were true, then many scenes I've been in would still be happening now, waiting and waiting for a laugh from the audience so my fellow players could edit it. If a scene is just over – laugh or not –- or if the players are due a stroke of mercy, the naked sweep edit can feel awkward in that it draws attention to the lack of laughter.

A soft edit is, well, soft. Like a cinematic cross fade, it attempts to blur the distinction between two moments. Hard edits include sweep edits (the cinematic equivalent of a cut to black and fade up) or a tag (which is more like a jump cut). Rather than having a player walk fully across the stage to sweep the scene and then turn to the play area, a soft edit involves a player simply entering the stage talking, initially to no one in particular. The onstage players complete the edit by leaving while an offstage player joins the initiator and their scene, now already in progress.

Here is an example of how a soft edit can look:

(Gary and Jenny are in a heated discussion)

Gary: Don't forget, he's your son too.

Jenny: My parents weren't stupid and neither am I. He must have gotten it from your side of the family.

Gary: Not fair! That is the most ridiculous –

(Eric enters from offstage. He begins speaking the moment he enters)

Eric: I've been looking over the sales numbers from last weekend. It appears ...

(Gary and Jenny leave the stage; Harry enters simultaneously)

Eric: ... that the bar did better business than the box office.

Harry: Lots of big drinkers on a Friday night.

Eric: I did the math. Each ticket sold was responsible for 134 dollars in bar sales.

Harry: Um ... that's a lot of top-shelf martinis.

Rather than talking, a player could enter a scene downstage center, actively disregarding the scene in progress and silently beginning an action or activity that tells everyone the current scene is over. Again, the other players notice the edit and leave or join as appropriate.

Direct address is another type of soft edit. This is the act of speaking directly to the audience to tell them what is happening or about to happen. Direct address can also be used to grease a tricky edit or provide a moment for a brief thematic move. A player takes the stage and tells the audience what they are seeing and how they should next focus their attention.

This example incorporates direct address into the bar scene between Eric and Harry:

Eric: Harry, I'm not stupid. You were managing that night. What happened?

Harry: What if I were to tell you that I dropped four bottles of gin, consecutively, while trying to make a gimlet and the patron that ordered it insisted on paying for all four bottles I broke?

Eric: I wouldn't believe you. Besides, it still would explain some but not all of the money the bar made.

Harry: What if I were to tell you it happened several times?

(Jo Ann enters from off stage, stands close to the side of the stage, and speaks directly to the audience.)

Jo Ann: This scene is taking place in a basement bar. One floor up is a dance studio.

(Diane and Tom take the stage and begin performing ballet stretches. Jo Ann leaves.)

Diane: Tonight's performance is going to be awesome. I can feel it.

French Scenes

A player may want to start a new scene in the same location of the current scene without involving any of the current characters. The solution is a French scene, a concept borrowed from the theater world.

The boundary between French scenes is the entrance or departure of a character or characters. If a scene is taking place in a coffee shop and an offstage actor wants to start a new scene in the same coffee shop, they could enter quietly and sit somewhere away from the current action. When they feel the time is right, they could begin speaking. This grabbing of the focus should communicate that the previous scene is over and a new one is beginning. Perhaps the actors in the previous scene don't leave but instead let go of the focus and just sit quietly, finishing their coffee.

There is no fixed mechanism (like tagging players or running in front of action) to beginning French scenes, and perhaps to preserve their elegance there shouldn't be. As with all soft editing techniques, we gain a moment of artistic expression where one would not have existed with a sweep edit, but we sacrifice clarity.

Transformations

A transformation edit is similar in feel to the classic improv exercise Freeze Tag. It uses a scene's stage picture as the starting point of another scene. Many times a group performing a Harold will use the visual of the opening and the last two actors onstage to begin the next scene. For example, say the opening ends with a narrated story telling of a tornado. The actors twirl about the stage, leaving one by one until there are two left. They stop spinning and plop down on the ground beginning the first scene with a line like, "No more dancing!" or "That party was amazing." A transformation can also occur between scenes. Perhaps a character is knocked unconscious and his lifeless body, sprawled on the ground, is used by the actors starting the next scene: "Shhh ... Honey, Griffin's asleep. You have his birthday presents?"

Beats

Plays have acts, baseball games have innings, books have chapters, and long form shows have beats. A short form show has clear starts and stops in the action, so it's easily segmented. The segments or beats in a long form show (or even in one long scene) can be trickier to identify. Most improv forms have some element of repetition built into them, and each of those complete laps forms a beat.

In the introduction I described a very simple form, one step more complicated than a montage, in which scenes would return as the show played out. In this form a beat would be each set of scenes that occurred before any of them were brought back.

Beats can also refer to segments of similar style or theme within a show or even a scene. Long scenes, like long conversations, move from topic to topic. Imagine you picked up an old friend from the airport.

The first beat of your conversation in the car could be called the "hand-shaking beat": *How are you, You look great, Let me help you with your bag.* The conversation might then move to the "big news beat": *You heard Tammy got divorced? I can't wait to see your kids, I moved out of that crummy apartment you saw last time you were here.* This could be followed, after brief silence, by a nostalgia beat: *Remember that time when ...?* It's one continuous scene that doesn't change location but could be divided into beats.

Second Beat Scenes and Callbacks

A second beat, or follow-on scene, is a scene that uses the characters, plot, or game of an earlier scene. Remember the first example scene I used at the start of this book, with Mary and Joe in the coffee shop? If a scene occurred later in that show with Mary explaining to her boss why she went on a two-hour coffee break, that would be the second beat of the original Mary and Joe coffee scene. The initiator intentionally starts the scene to recall the Mary and Joe scene.

While plot and character are the most obvious things to use to create a second beat scene, they're not the only things. The game of a scene can also recur completely divorced of the specifics of the scene it originated from. The Mary and Joe coffee shop scene had a general agreement game ("I'm sooo misunderstood"/"You're soooo misunderstood") that could inspire a follow-on scene with Mary going back to her office. But we could also see Mary with her boyfriend. Does she treat him the same way she does her boss, with snotty indifference? We could also see her boss looking around the office for her. Perhaps the other employees are making up flimsy excuses for her long lunch break.

We could also see her boss on a coffee break with another boss complaining about his employees. In fact, it doesn't even have to be Mary's boss for a bosses-griping general-agreement scene to work. We could also lose the specifics of the scene and see a second beat scene about two astronauts on the moon complaining about mission control ("What control freaks") while drinking Tang. The point is that the initiator of the scene intentionally uses the first scene as direct inspiration for their scene. Can there be third and fourth beats of a scene? Sure, why not?

What's the Most Important Part of Any Scene?

Here's a hint: It isn't the plot. Asked a different way, what aspect of the scene carries the burden of its identity? It isn't *what* is going on but *who* is going on. How different of a movie would *Taxi Driver* be if Travis Bickle wasn't a taxi driver but the new guy working in the mail room of a business? If Iris and Sport weren't prostitute and pimp but dominated secretary and maniacal boss? As long as Travis is still an unstable man with no history, fighting against what he sees as injustice, the movie will be very similar.

If you really want to change *Taxi Driver*, rather than changing the specifics of what's going on, you have to change *who* is going on. Imagine if Travis, back to being a taxi driver, was instead a Jeffrey "The Dude" Lebowski type: a lazy, aging, former hippie radical. Now we have a very different movie. The chances of him buying an arsenal of guns is zero. He'd probably quit the moment he has to clean up various bodily fluids from the back of his cab.

The context, while required, is simply an excuse for the characters to exist. It can be changed and molded without altering much of a scene's identity. But if we change a character's behavior, we get a different scene. Therefore a scene is defined by the "who." When doing second beats or scenes inspired by other scenes, you'll get better mileage by looking not just at what could happen, but what could happen to whom.

A second-beat scene refers to an entire scene inspired by a previous scene. But when only one detail of a previous scene is used in another scene, it's called a callback. Once the notion of a coffee break lasting two hours has happened, any other scene can pick it up and use it. A scene about two hungry soldiers fighting over the last piece of fresh fruit could have the sergeant arriving and apologizing for not being available because he was on a two-hour coffee break. The only similarity between that scene and the previous scene is the notion of a two-hour coffee break.

Characters, single bits of information, and concepts (like the concept of all coffee breaks lasting two hours) are commonly used as callbacks in other scenes. While they are fun, and provide cool cross-pollination between different scene threads, they can be done too early or forced in where they don't fit. It isn't uncommon for groups to have stylistic house rules about when callbacks and second beats are allowed and when they're discouraged.

Uncle Owen and Aunt Beru

About 15 minutes into the movie *Star Wars*, a young farm boy, Luke Skywalker, is having breakfast with his adoptive aunt and uncle. He wants to go to space academy and they want him to stay on the farm. Luke gets angry and leaves in a huff. What happens later in the movie? Do his aunt and uncle have a change of heart? Does Luke leave a note for them and run away? Do they have a tear-jerking reconciliation scene at the end of the movie?

No. (Spoiler alert) Luke sees Uncle Owen and Aunt Beru ten minutes later ... as charred corpses. Just because you played a character in the first beat of a show does not mean you automatically are the star of the rest of the show. You could be Uncle Owen or Aunt Beru.

A Generic Form

It can be daunting to dive into this form-designing business with a blank sheet of paper. Let's start with a simple base form that's at the heart of most Chicago-style forms. Well-known shows like Harold, Asssscat, and Whirled News are each unique and successful in their own right, yet underneath the differences is the same prototype structure, based on the following elements.

> Suggestion: A word or phrase from the audience.

> Source: A game or group scene, inspired by the suggestion, which provides information.

> Deconstruction: Scenes that take their inspiration from the source.

> Reset: A recursive device that marks the beginning and end of beats and can act as a new source for the next beat.

Now we've got all the tools we'll need: scenes, games, connecting bits, and show techniques. By selecting how each of these segments will be played, you can easily create your own forms. Let's explore this skeletal structure. After all, it's the "form" in "long form."

The Suggestion

Most (but not all) long form shows begin by asking for a suggestion from the audience. Some shows ask the audience for a particular type of suggestion – "Someone shout out the worst present you ever got for

Christmas" or "What was the name of the last person that broke your heart?"

It may be integral to the show to get a particular type of suggestion. Perhaps your show needs a suggestion of a country in the world because the form starts with a scene paint of a trophy gallery filled with objects from that country. Perhaps your form begins with a full cast scene, so you need the suggestion of a location that could reasonably include all eight people. This is sometimes called the "get," as in "We need to make sure our get tells the audience what type of suggestion we need for our show."

Before you start trying to think of some cool get, remember to be careful what you ask for. Too interesting or too funny a get and you risk making a promise to the audience about how hilarious or interesting your show will be that you may not be able to fulfill.

Sometimes gets are too complicated:

> "For our suggestion, we just need the feeling you got the last time you met someone that is a friend of a friend of yours but you hadn't met them yet ... within the last week."

or too narrow:

> "Someone shout out a room in a typical office. Break room? We've already gotten that one. Copier room? Again, we got that one last week. Boss's office? If you came to our shows regularly you'd know that we've already had that suggestion two or three times!"

I'm fond of asking the audience for anything at all, free of qualifiers: "May we have a suggestion of anything at all." It doesn't set any expectations ... except perhaps a sense that you're brave to give so much power to the audience!

Some players are quick to blame a bad suggestion for a bad show ... but they rarely credit a good suggestion with a good show. Don't give so much power to the suggestion. In reality, unless your show hits the suggestion on the head throughout, the audience will forget what it was. You could even argue that it's a vestigial remnant of improv's past.

How close does your show need to stay to the suggestion? Depends on the form. In general, the suggestion is there to suggest the first move and perhaps to be referred to later. As an improviser, once that first move is made, it's your job to support it and press forward, not think of artificial ways to cram the suggestion back into the show.

You may feel that the suggestion is there to prove the show is improvised, and for some audience members it performs that function. But don't take the challenge of having to prove to the audience that the show is truly improvised too seriously. I've seen many shows flounder because rather than playing in the moment and truly improvising, the actors are playing out of fear that the audience doesn't believe they're making it up, or will be upset if they don't see how the suggestion is being used.

The Suggestion in a Theoretical Sense

Why take a suggestion in the first place? When I was first exposed to improv (on the TV show *Whose Line is It Anyway?* and at SAK Theater in Orlando) I was fascinated by the ability of the players to take anything given to them and effortlessly create something funny from it. The players were so witty and at ease. I got the feeling that they could do anything and the suggestions were just hurdles for them to clear. Taking a suggestion was almost challenge to the audience: "Give us your best shot!"

Once I got involved in short form improv and started getting suggestions thrown at me, I began to resent the audience. I wanted to tell them that I was an interesting and funny person, and that if they quit trying to make me jump through hoops, they'd see it, too. But they came to improv shows expecting us to use whatever wacky suggestions they could come up with. Perhaps my frustration was with my assumptions about suggestions. Besides, don't we have to demonstrate that it's truly improvised? Why else would they come? There was satisfaction when the audience got to see how their suggestions were used. They felt invested in the show. The suggestion went from being a challenge to a string that binds the audience to the players: "The show you are about to see is improvised and we need your help to do it."

Long form was a different beast. The suggestion took on more importance in that it informed the whole show. But since only one was taken, the notion of improv as an interactive experience that required audience participation was gone. Players were no longer graded on how creatively they used the suggestion. Many shows began to deviate quite dramatically from the suggestion. Did audiences complain about that fact? Not really. If the show was good, they enjoyed it for what it was, a piece of spontaneous theater. The suggestion was referred to as a springboard or a starting point: "We just need one suggestion to get our show rolling."

There is a very popular show in Chicago starring two of the city's most talented players, T.J. Jagadowski and Dave Pasquesi, and they don't take a suggestion. Not asking for a suggestion is breaking the last thread that connected improv to its theater game past. It's now an art to be judged on its own merit. Improv no longer has to be a showcase for the witty, or a place for an audience to try to stump the players. In truth, a person can improvise successfully without any input from the audience. By not taking a suggestion, T.J. and Dave say to their audiences, "If you don't believe it's improvised, fine. We won't compromise our show to try to convince you otherwise." These feelings are explained in the words they use to start their show: "Trust us, this is all made up."

The Source

The source is what happens immediately after the suggestion. It is typically preset – not the content, but the game to be performed. The source could be a classic Harold opening (complex game), a player reading a real newspaper article, a player giving a monologue inspired by the suggestion, a song played at random from an audience member's iPod, a slice-of-life group scene, a long two-player scene (emphasizing behavior over a scene game), an improvised song, a press conference (or any similar game), an audience member telling a story, an audience member drawing a tarot card, or the players asking each other questions. You've got options. While its job is to inspire the team and get them thinking together, it shouldn't be played with the intent to inspire, which can come across as pretentious. It should be played honestly, the players trusting that it will be inspirational.

Deconstruction

Big word, but it simply means performing scenes inspired by the source. It doesn't mean replaying the source scene. It means taking it apart and doing scenes inspired by the pieces. While doing the opening, what struck you as cool or funny? Do a scene about it. (There is a form called the Deconstruction, with a capital D, that asks the players to attack the source in very specific ways through scene work and, yes, it also follows this generic form).

Reset

The reset can be a scene, group scene, or game that has a different energy from the scenes. The difference in energy signifies to the players and audience that something new is about to begin. Examples of resets might be bringing back the opening device (perhaps continuing a monologue or group scene used to open the show) or using a new long form game to explore something uncovered in the show so far. They may involve the whole cast or a few players. Some forms define how many scenes happen before the reset (e.g., three in a three-scenes-game Harold) while others leave that decision to the players in the show.

Putting It Together

Let's put on a show! It would be cool if the show started with a full-cast group scene and then if after a few minutes one player is selected as "it" and gets character painted. Then the deconstruction scenes follow that character through life from childhood until death. For the reset, the actors that played the people in "it"s life give character monologue eulogies at the funeral and a new "it" is selected. I've got two words for that form: good and luck.

Sorry for the "gotcha!" but the form above puts a tremendous burden on the players, who already are being asked to make up everything as they go along ... yet it sounds fun. If the audience picks up on what's happening, they may get a warm fuzzy, but if the scenes themselves are boring or forced, the audience won't be engaged. Improv scenes are at their best when unrestricted by predetermined plot and given the freedom to discover themselves. An interesting or cool-sounding form is often a prison for the players, who are forced to play from a place of obligation, making choices out of fear of doing it wrong and ruining the show. The best forms are the ones that don't force cool onto the players but instead allow them to discover it as they play.

A simpler form might be this: Get a suggestion from the audience of anything at all. The source is a press conference inspired by that suggestion. The scenes that follow consist of the actors deconstructing the press conference.

After three or four scenes, an actor steps forward and gives a truthful monologue inspired by something in the show so far. That monologue inspires more scenes, with another round or two of monologues after several scenes.

Perhaps the show could end, after 25 minutes, with the press conference returning to discuss a new idea, or bringing back the old one. It will take practice for the actors to figure out where the end should be. You could number all of the scenes (two scenes per beat, split by monologues for four beats), or you could just feel your way through.

The power of this form is its simplicity. The content of the scenes isn't prescribed by the form but rather is up to the players. (In the form example I gave about going to "It"'s funeral, scene content was determined by the form). The form provides structure and time marking only, giving power to the players.

> **Best Laid Plans ...**
>
> Harvey Littleton, father of the studio art glass movement and mentor to Dale Chihuly, famously said, "Technique is cheap." I'm not sure how much you paid for this book, but that amount is exactly how much this set of techniques costs. All the technique in the world gives no clues as to what one should create with it. The spirit of creation, the need to make real, the compulsion to step onstage with a few friends armed only with your honesty cannot be purchased.
>
> Friction can arise between players who embrace this spirit and those who cling mercilessly to one style or the other. Or those who feel that if they just take one more class, they'll finally have earned the right to perform. Please take classes, please buy my book, but know that if we are to consider improv art, then you have to be an artist. Go create and be proud of what you create.

How Does It End?

While some forms have built-in mechanisms to end them, many do not. Typically, shows last 25 to 35 minutes, with a director or trusted individual running lights and calling the end of the show with a light pull (i.e., a blackout). This is a straightforward approach for forms with engineered endings. The advice I give for forms that do not have a set end device is to try to end the show on game energy (a capping monologue or group game), as opposed to a scene. Unless the final scene features the whole cast, and its content is some climactic event, it can be awkward to just have the lights go out in a seemingly random place. While a form may not have a preset ending device, many, when played well, do converge on a simple plot point and/or theme. The players should embrace this and encourage it to happen.

5.

SAMPLE FORMS

How You Play Determines What You Get
I hope this point has sunk in by now: There are so many right ways to play and how you play determines what you get. Which of the improv rules are you going to honor and which are you going to forget about? This determines the feel and pace of your show. As long form players, you're also directors. You get to choose the style of your show. If as players you ruthlessly yes-and and avoid taking positions against each other, then we won't get any conflict scenes. If that's your artistic vision, awesome. If you want conflict scenes– truthful conflict – in your shows, you can't also blindly yes-and and avoid asking questions. Once you know the kind of show you want to do, go back and pick the improv scene rules that make that kind of show happen.

The next section includes sample forms you can try for yourself. The first four are simple, boiled-down forms that make wonderful starting points for customization. (I've given them long, awkward names to encourage this!) The last form, Detours, is fully realized and uses a unique conceit. It's included to demonstrate that an apparently dumb idea, like doing one scene over and over again, can be used to create a fantastic form if you dive in and give it a go. Try them. Keep what you like, discard the rest. Find what works best for you. Notice that I said "find" and not "think about." The only way to know what works is to try it.

If you're a short form player experimenting with long form, know that you have actually done some long form already. Short form games like Day in the Life, The Dream, and Improvised Musical consist of multiple scenes and require the players to edit and move the action around without any input from a host. I've used the term "mid form" to describe these long short form games, games with a firm conceit and multiple scenes in which the players control the flow of action.

No Form Police

No one will ever tell you you're doing it wrong. You may not have success with a particular form, but don't confuse doing something poorly with doing it incorrectly. Plenty of groups do shows that are both correct and boring. I've had many students play from a place of wanting to get things right, as if Del Close Zeus will step down from Mount Improv Olympus and give them an award for doing it properly. The audience does not have (and should not need) an improv checklist with all the rules. They don't come to check your homework. They come to see you create.

Saying there is no form police isn't just about not playing to impress your teachers and directors. When I tell my students there's no

156

form police, many of them think, "Oh good, no one will arrest me when I screw up." What I want them to think is, "There's no police? Let's go rob a bank!"

Montage

This the simplest form. It can be done without even having a source beat. It can be as long or as short as you want and include any number of people. The form consists simply of getting a suggestion, then doing scenes inspired by that suggestion, one after the other. You can engineer gimmicks into the form by having the first three scenes be fairly short and played with big, broad characters before slowing the pace (by mellowing the style of play) for the rest of the show. Look to place group scenes or games (resets) throughout the form for a change of pace, and to act as energy bumps.

As a group you can decide if and when walk-ons, callbacks, cut-tos, and tag-outs are legal. These moves tend to accelerate pace and burn through ideas quickly, so while they would be legal from the start in a fast-paced show, you may wish to hold off on them for a slower-paced show. While I imagine most groups would want all those things in their shows, it's important to come to a soft understanding about when in the show they are legal, and when they are not. If you're aiming for a 25-minute-plus show, you may want to limit those moves to reset moments and perhaps the end, so that the show concludes in a run. When I coach montages I give this general advice:

- You may find the lack of a form to be both liberating and challenging. The challenge is that the lack of structure can give players cold feet about creating new scenes. Scene initiations tend to slide from thought-about and purposeful to random and as the show goes along. That's fine. Don't let the lack of a well-formed scene idea prevent you from editing and starting a new scene.

- While players can have difficulty continuing to create new ideas off of that first suggestion, the pace can also draw down the physical energy. As the show goes along, worry less about being true to the suggestion and more about keeping the energy up. Get out and play.

Monologue Deconstruction

Many improv theaters around the country (around the world, actually) present a monologue deconstruction as part of their regular show lineup. It's a simple form that allows players some freedom in how they choose to use the source material (both relationship and game scenes are acceptable). The source material is monologues (typically truthful) that provide inspiration for performing scenes. The monologues also provide a good change of pace and energy from the scenes.

While each theater may have different house rules, they're essentially playing the same form. The source and resets consist of a monologist taking the stage to tell true stories. The scenes are inspired by the monologues.

Players often feel that if the audience can't immediately see what has been taken from the monologue to inspire a scene, they won't "get it." Unless you feel strongly about clear and direct inspiration from the monologues being a part of your show, it's not absolutely necessary. An engaging scene, inspired by the monologue but not in an obvious way, will trump any nagging sense of not understanding where a scene came from in the audience's mind.

As far as who gives the monologues, it could be a cast member picked before the show or a local personality arranged in advance. I've seen police officers, musicians, city council members, and people with interesting jobs serve as monologists. I've even seen monologists engage the audience with a Q and A during a show. Some general notes:

- This form breeds many scene initiations of the "follow me" type, with an initiating player proposing a firm scene idea. Respect the initiator. Avoid cross-initiations. You may yes without anding until you understand what the initiator's going for or decide that they didn't have a firm idea after all. (Maybe give them three or four lines to get their idea across.)

- Don't hold on to your inspiration from the monologue so tightly that you forget to play the scene you're actually in. You won't be graded on what your inspiration was or how well you used it.

- Consider holding onto callbacks and second beats until the end of the show. A typical group will get three or four beats in a 25 minute show. The last beat can be a high-energy run with callbacks, second beats, walk-ons, and tag-outs.

Group Scene Nothing Happens

This form is not defined by the order the scenes are in but by the style of play required to make the form work. It uses the generic source-deconstruct-reset structure, with the scenes in the deconstruct beat inspired by what happens in a full-cast group scene. While scenes make up both the source and deconstruct beats, they're played with very different rules. The deconstructed scenes may include wild ideas, frustration games, and characters playing against each other. The group scene, however, is played so that nothing happens.

By "nothing happens," I mean that the situation that has brought everyone together, and what transpires as a result, will be somewhat unremarkable. A scene with nothing remarkable happening may sound like slow improv death, but when played well, these conflict-wary relationship scenes are fun to play, fun to watch, and – most importantly for this form – full of information. A long car ride with friends is unremarkable but can be tremendous fun. That's what these scenes are, in essence: road trips with friends that the audience gets to observe.

For the group scene's context I tend to favor simple, as-seen-in-life situations: a group of friends hanging out on a hotel balcony during spring break, the waitstaff of a restaurant doing their sidework after it's closed, or guests at a backyard barbecue. As in life, once we've established how sweet this balcony overlooking spring break is in the first three lines, the conversation will move away from it onto whatever things are affecting those characters' lives. Tell stories. Ask questions. It's friends hanging out.

Who decides what is and what isn't remarkable? The players do, according to how they improvise the scene: specifically, what they react to and how big they choose to make those reactions. A group of friends waiting outside a concert venue might seem like an unremarkable situation, but if one player chooses to get really emotional (and inconsolable) about a perceived insult, then it becomes remarkable. These scenes aren't "that day when Jerry flipped his lid and almost punched Doug," they're "that day when Jerry flipped out and everyone laughed, even Jerry, after a while."

The job of the source scene is to explore. The reason for avoiding extended conflict and game-scene energy is that they both tend to narrow the focus of a scene onto one point and keep it there until it's resolved. These group scenes unfold much like our lives. Conversations ebb and flow and the person who's the center of attention one moment won't be the next. If something comes up that should get a rise out of somebody, that person can push back a little, but then they have to shrug it off or accept it and ask everyone to move on, which everyone else must then do.

No Thanksgiving Disasters, Please!

I feel like a mom with young children when I tell my students that they're going to do a Thanksgiving dinner scene but to please behave. More often than not, these scenes end up being examples of unimaginably dysfunctional families. The father is an alcoholic tyrant, the daughter is a pansexual fascist-feminist, the son is a pyromaniac/cutter/chronic masturbator, the grandfather is a racist with bladder and/or bowel control problems, and poor mom tries to hold things together. I've seen it a million times! Why is this family still celebrating Thanksgiving together? All that craziness must be addressed by the players, which given its extreme forms will undoubtedly lead to arguments. Any one of those absurdities is more than enough for several Group Scene Nothing Happens scenes.

Some groups make it a rule that their show will always take place in a predefined place like an office break room or a car on a road trip. If you choose to define the location and circumstance improvisationally, don't be afraid to be bold when defining the situation and your role in it. If the players aren't perfectly sure where they are and what's going on, they'll struggle to provide information, for fear of ruining something. While a line like "How cool is it that we got everyone from the office to fit in this hot tub?" is very heavy-handed, it does an outstanding job of letting everyone know what's going on, opening the door for other people to improvise freely.

In this form, players open with a group scene, edit it internally, and then perform scenes inspired by the group scene. Teams typically revisit the same group situation and characters for the reset moments, although the reset moments could also be anything else. Some groups have a standing rule that if the group scene is going very well it should not be edited, and therefore it could potentially become the entire show. Or it could be edited near the end of the show and followed by a quick run of inspired scenes played with high energy.

Everyone Knows What's Going On But Me

This is a common thought in the minds of players during a show. You may be standing on the side watching, unable to follow the action or understand why people are laughing. The truth is that if you're thinking that, the majority of your fellow players are too. Rarely – and usually with hilarious and/or disastrous results – does a single player get terribly out of sync with the team. What is far more common than one person being lost is that everyone is lost.

Here are some things to think about:

- When returning to the group scene, be careful of introducing the notion that some large plot point has occurred since we last saw the scene. Can time have passed? Yes. Might something have occurred since we last saw the scene? Certainly. But if it's too big a story jump, it runs the risk of taking over the scene.

- Lines that encourage input from everyone and that prevent getting fixated for too long on one person, such as "Let's all go around the room and name our favorite 80's sitcom and why," may seem cheap and blunt but in spirit they can create the right kind of environment.

- It's easy for the group scene to feature one character who is a total contrarian. Be careful about doing that. Why would they be there in the first place? You may play against, but instead of being 180 degrees opposed, try being only 90 degrees opposed. There will be at least one topic about which you can feel the same way the group does. Rather than against, play askew.

Same General, Different Specific

This is another bare-bones form that's at the heart of some other more intricate forms (Close Quarters, a classic of the iO Theater, being one). The central premise is that all the scenes take place in specific areas within the same general location. The scenes involve specific people you might expect to find in those locations. For instance, if the general location is a diner, some specific areas might be the counter, a booth, and the grill. Some specific people you might find in those areas could include the old regular and the kind waitress at the counter; two high school sweethearts sharing a malted in the booth, or the cranky short-order cook and the sassy waitress at the grill.

These scenes are played with an eye toward keeping things real. Maybe there's something strange or out-of-whack about the scenes, but it should be possible to conceive all of them taking place in a diner. It's important to your fellow players to know specifically who and where you are, so be very clear with your character and location choices. Don't be afraid to play archetypal characters.

Because this form relies on two- to five-minute relationship scenes, game scenes – especially group game scenes – make for strong reset choices. To continue the diner example, a group reset could be the manager calling a meeting in the supply room to tell the staff there's been a rash of customers leaving without paying their bills. It could be played press conference style.

As with other bare-bones forms, there's some wiggle room to add house rules to Same General, Different Specific and make it your own. When I do this form in workshops, I use these special rules:

-No bringing back sub-locations or people (this makes it more of a brainstorming exercise.) Actors can play different characters.

-Don't feel obligated to reference other scenes or characters in your scene. If we learn in the first scene that the diner is closing for business next week, please ignore that fact in your scene.

-After 15 or 20 minutes I lift the no call back restriction. Players may call back people, sub-locations and plot points from other scenes, but they're not required to.

-When the show has five minutes left, the players must start a fast-paced run. Any unused ideas, callbacks, or wild premises are now legal. The players should be more concerned with maintaining a fast, fun pace than with scene content.

For a suggestion, you could ask for a specific location. (Careful, you might get similar suggestions over the course of several shows). You can also ask for a suggestion of anything and then let the first scene define the space for you.

Jocks, Nerds, and Preppies at Their Lockers

If you think playing archetypes is cheap or gauche, please know it is much simpler to start with an archetype and find nuance early in a scene than it is to expect to have a completely layered character with wants and needs and subtext ready to go at line one. I typically tell my students that I need to be able to write who you are and where you are on a Post-it note. "Sleazy traveling salesman" and "Snarky waiter at the cash register" would fit nicely. "Kind of

too old to still be working as a busboy but full
of life experience, though he has a dark side,
standing around the side of the building near
the Dumpsters, but also in earshot of the front
door" does not fit on a Post-it note. Start with
an archetype, then discover texture.

Detours

A Discovered Form

As a form, Detours started with the first team I played with at iO, People of Earth. Our coach, Peter Gwinn, brought in an exercise that worked so well with us that we turned it into a form. The exercise and the core skill of the form involves two actors replaying a two-to-three-minute scene just played by two other actors. Their job was to not only do the best they could to replay the scene, but to also follow any organic changes that occurred. Rather than busting each other for a missed line – "Didn't you mean to say that you were hungry?" – the actors play the scene they are in, play with their partner and use the original scene as a road map.

It was a great exercise on its own, and we started doing two or three or four replays per scene and had a blast interpreting and reinterpreting each others' characters and choices. The form and the road map/travel analogies eventually led to the name Detours. It's the kind of form that could have only been discovered. If someone brought it in and explained it to us – play the exact scene over and over again for twenty minutes – it never would have happened.

Detours is a form in which one and only one scene is performed over and over again. We never see what happens before the scene or what happens after the scene. No new characters are introduced. Fifteen to 20 minutes of the same scene over and over and over again. It sounds ridiculous. But it's very fun to play once you grasp its peculiarities.

The show starts with a player asking for a suggestion of anything and then leaving the stage. Two players enter and perform a scene for at least three minutes. It is played as a relationship scene rather than a game scene. Since it is part of the source, it needs to be vivid and full of detail.

The second scene (the first replay) is initiated by an offstage player tagging out an onstage player. The scene starts at the beginning, with the new player taking over the role of the player they tagged out. This scene is played as close to the source as possible while still being conversational and in-the-moment. After this scene, a new player enters and tags out the remaining original player. The scene goes back to the beginning and is replayed a second time. This run of three scenes – the "zero scene" and its two replays – comprises the source beat. (While the zero scene may be three plus minutes, the first two replays move more efficiently. Don't worry about blowing nine minutes just to get to this point.)

What follows next are more replays, but now the actors are encouraged to make willful changes. They have the road map and can explore some detours. Some examples of typical detours are:

- Altering a character's behavior or changing a specific reaction.

- Exaggerating an innocent moment in the source scene until it's ridiculous.

- Changing a key noun at the end of a sentence. This typically begins a tag-out run. Standard tag-out rules apply (for example, if you're left onstage, you're still the same character.)

Here are the first few moments of a source scene (which would typically run three to five minutes):

(Two actors pantomime that they are gardening. One actor stands and approaches the other, resting her arms on an imaginary fence)

Jordan (very friendly and folksy): Working in the garden, huh?

Ed (also friendly): You too!

Jordan: It's a beautiful day. A bit hot, but what can you do?

Ed: I've been meaning to ask you about your roses.

Jordan: You wanna talk flowers?

Ed: My roses bud but don't open. Thoughts?

Jordan: My flowers love bone meal fertilizer.

That's the source. After the two replays (which stay loyal to the source scene), a new player sweeps the scene, takes on the Jordan role, and starts from the beginning.

Jordan (sexy): Working in the garden, huh?

Ed (very nervous): You too?

Jordan (fans herself, pantomimes unbuttoning her shirt): It's a beautiful day. A bit hot, but what can you do?

Ed (still very nervous): I've been meaning to ask you about your roses. Perhaps another time.

Jordan: You wanna talk flowers, huh?

(A new player tags out Ed)

Ed (hyper-macho and confident): My roses bud but don't open. Thoughts?
Jordan: My flower loves bone ... meal fertilizer.

(A new player tags out Jordan)

Jordan: My flower loves dinner and a movie.

(Another player tags out Jordan)

Jordan: My flower loves long walks on the beach.

(Another player tags out Jordan)

Jordan (snarky and un-sexy): I'm not going to have sex with you.

(The scene is swept. Two new actors take the stage as Jordan and Ed)

Jordan (folksy and friendly, as in the source scene): Working in the garden, huh?

Ed (agitated and sarcastic): You too?

Jordan (oblivious to Ed's bad attitude): It's a beautiful day. A bit hot, but what can you do?

Ed: I've been meaning to ask you to shut up.

Those are examples of some non-organic, follow-me-type detours and the tag-outs they might inspire. The reset for this form is to sweep the scene and begin a replay where the actors do not bring in any changes but instead follow any organic changes that occur naturally. This results in a slower scene and allows the actors a chance to refresh their memories about the source.

Here is some general advice for performing this form:

-Try to keep the first three lines of the source intact throughout. It will help anchor the scene and, through repetition, communicate to the audience that you are replaying the same scene.

-Scenes can start from deeper points inside the source scene. The above example was too short to illustrate this, but a player could sweep and start their scene in the middle of the source scene. Since scenes don't typically last very long before they are tagged into or edited, this gives the players fresh ammunition for their scenes.

-Resets are played as straight, honest replays of the source. This form can generate some high-paced tag runs and burn through ideas quickly. Rather than forcing ideas that may not work, a player may always simply replay the source honestly and allow the moment to inspire changes.

When I teach the form, I start with the old Peter Gwinn exercise of replaying scenes, giving everyone a chance to honestly replay each other's scenes. Again, when the actors are unable to exactly reproduce the source scene, they're instructed to play the moment and follow the new scene, casually looking for moments to get back on track. Don't be afraid to detour, but recognize that you still need to go the same place the original scene went. This type of honest replay, used in both the source and reset, is a critical skill needed to make this form work.

CONCLUSIONS

I started this book with an analogy comparing my arrival in Chicago and discovering improv as like finding cool stuff in my brother's closet when he went off to college. In truth I have an older sister and she left NOTHING of interest in her closet when she went off to school. She had nothing of interest to me in her closet when she lived at home, for that matter. So perhaps for me, personally, it's a poor analogy.

I also think it's a poor analogy in another respect. An older brother's closet is full of tokens of the past. Once they leave for school, nothing will ever be added to it. This book, however, is full of my own thoughts, theories and exercises. Writing this has forced me to look back over my career, separate the noise from the signal, and commit to paper what I believe to be true. In a roundabout sort of way, the Five Assumptions are actually Five Conclusions; for you they may be new but for me they are the end result of, after years of teaching, asking myself, "What things am I constantly telling my students?"

- Playing the simple reality that your scene presents to you is always a strong and correct choice.
- You don't need a funny first line or funny response to have a successful scene.
- Provide clear details. If your partner isn't being clear, ask them for details.
- Truthfully portray the person involved in the funny idea, premise, or conceit.
- Rather than playing to satisfy the rules, play the moment wherever it takes you. *Anything can happen.*

I have to reiterate the point I made in the first shaded area section in the introduction: style is a subset of technique. If you follow the techniques in this book it will birth a particular style of play. I hope you find this style fun, refreshing, and expansive in the type of scenes it allows. This style is my best attempt to make the following phrase a reality: if it happens in life it can happen on stage. That's been my primary thought for the last decade. If improv is to be considered the equal of scripted work it must leave behind the concepts and rules that limit it to a subset of life's experiences.

I also hope these techniques are easy to digest, implement, and make second nature. We shouldn't take the knowledge and wisdom of others onstage with us, we should take ourselves onstage and trust that whatever we've learned is inside of us. It can be difficult to clear our heads, and for that I'd like to close with the final passage from *The Compleat Angler*, a passage which is equally good advice for the fisherman or the improviser:

"Study to be quiet."
Izaak Walton, *The Compleat Angler*, 1653

Exercises

Simple Scenes

The ability to live in a scene, portraying the simple reality of the characters, helps a player relax and find rather than force humor.

Explanation:
Two actors take the stage. The designated initiator starts the scene with a line taken from real life. Not an interesting or spectacular line, just a line. "Here are those reports you wanted," "The groceries are out in the car," "I made meatloaf for dinner." The actors are to play the simple reality that their lines imply, reacting and speaking as they feel a typical person would in life. These scenes may feature crying or laughing or anger or sadness. If this was really happening, how would I react? As the scene progresses, one or both actors may find that a pattern of behavior, a character, is developing. They should worry less about playing as a typical person and more about continuing to play this new character.

Coaching Points:
- Coach this with an eye toward reality. If you don't believe what you're seeing, say so. If the players don't say exactly what they are seeing on their partners, ask them to. "You look tired," "You're angry," and "I can see

you're frustrated" are the kinds of lines you should be hearing from them.

- Sometimes actors confuse being real with being intense. Their responses should be commensurate with the stimuli. If someone says, "But in real life I'd scream at that guy," and you feel it was too intense of a choice, remind them of the context of the scene they are in. Are they in public? Is this person a stranger? These are things that can temper strong emotions.

- Actors can get too glossy or emotionally unavailable. If they're pinched, they must say ouch. Reacting, saying ouch, doesn't need to be some huge, emotional outburst but it must recognize and acknowledge the moment and whatever information was conveyed in the emotions of their partner and not just the words used.

- Actors are not always forthcoming with details. If you hear generalities – "You always do that," "I'm so tired," "I have the worst boss ever" – ask them to explain. The juror needs evidence. "I'm so tired; I woke up at 5:30 because my cat attacked my face," "I have the worst boss ever. He's making us come in on Saturday and pretend to be him if anyone calls so he doesn't miss the opening of muskie season." Train your actors to question their partners if they hear vagaries.

Variations:
-People You Know: The actors portray specific people from their lives, worrying more about playing their behaviors (greedy, overly friendly, slow talker) and less about playing their vocation or role (garbage collector, mom, college professor).

-Silent Start: Starting in silence with the actors pantomiming for several moments before speaking.

Emotional Noise

Many improvisers have fallen in love with wordplay and verbal wit, and as a result they may come across as bland and lifeless onstage. Even the most tight-lipped Victorian colonel sitting in his richly appointed drawing room might occasionally clear his throat briefly to show his impatience with a clueless servant. Emotions say more than words. We are told to care about what is going on. Giving an emotional response is how an actor cares.

Explanation:
Two actors onstage. The designated initiator is to initiate verbally with a simple, slice-of-life line of dialogue. The responder, before saying any words, must make an emotional noise that expresses how he feels about the initiation. The emotional noise could also be an exclamation – "Hey!" "Oh no!" – a hearty laugh, an evil laugh, a sexy-come-hither "Oh,"an exhale, a giddy "Wheeee," or a "Harrumph" with pursed lips. Once the initiator has made her noise, she may speak if she chooses. The scene continues with neither actor required to make any emotional noises.

Coaching Points:
- The responder should not bring in any emotional, physical, or object choices. He should just stand patiently and listen to the initiator.

- The initiator should avoid first lines that beg a specific emotion, like "My dog is sick," or "I want a divorce." A line like "You mind if we take my car?" is preferred.

- The responder might gloss over, forget, or quickly downplay their emotional response. Make sure that the initial response is a distinct choice that's audible and visible on the face and/or body and that it isn't tossed away.

- The initiator may focus more on the words of the responder and not the noise. The noise is more important than the words and must be acknowledged by the initiator.

Variations:

-Only Noise: The responder doesn't get a line following their noise. The initiator must speak again, reacting to the noise before the scene continues with dialogue.

-Blind Emotional Noise: The responder puts his fingers in his ears, hums to himself, and turns away from the initiator. The initiator says her initiation out loud. The director points to the "deaf" and "blind" responder, who must immediately make a noise, having not heard the initiation. He then removes his fingers from his ears and turns to the initiator, who re-initiates the scene with the same line. The responder responds with the same noise he made while "blind." This may create some very absurd and interesting juxtapositions.

-Restate Initiation: The responder's first line of dialogue does not have to be preceded by an emotional noise. Their first line, however, can only consist of words from the initiator's line. They may change an "I" to a "you," as "I love ice cream" may become "You love ice cream." Words can also be omitted to maintain conversational dialogue. While a word or two may be added, no new thoughts may be included. The responder must, however, make a strong choice as to how they say their line of dialogue and the initiator must respond to it. Angry, elated, dejected, relieved, disgusted – it doesn't matter. The scene may continue as normal after the first exchange.

With and Against

An actor's character does not need to be accepting of the other character's actions. As long as the actors agree to the circumstances, we can have a scene. Any well-played reaction, be it positive or negative, can create just as good a scene as any other can. A character may choose to be "with" the other character and be happy, giddy, reassuring, polite yet reserved, ecstatic, or aroused. He may also play "against" and be unhappy, disappointed, embarrassed, cold, or disgusted, or cry, or force a laugh.

Explanation:
A two-person scene is started by a designated initiator. The responder and the coach are to pay special attention to how he responds to the first line. Is he happy or unhappy to hear that line? Cool or uncool with what's going on? After 30 to 90 seconds, the scene is replayed. The same initiation is given, but the responder is to take an alternate path with his response. If he was happy to hear the initiation, he's now unhappy. If he was not cool with what was happening, now he's cool with it. He was with; now he's against. "Cool" and "uncool" both encompass worlds of possible choices.

Coaching Points:
- Some responders may feel uncomfortable playing against and may couch their choices in niceness, spoonful-of-sugar style. Remind them of the locker ask-out scene I described. Not every date request gets an okay, but that doesn't mean you have to be rude.

- Some initiators (the *actor*), when faced with an against, acquiesce and defuse the situation rather than feeling the hurt or pain or embarrassment.

The *character* may attempt to defuse the situation, but she mustn't lose her hurt or embarrassment or whatever emotion she felt when their partner played against.

- Some actors have a natural tendency to play against. Make sure that when they play with, they play truly and show honest emotions. These actors might say yes to the date request but then play the scene coldly, keeping their partner physically and emotionally at arm's length.

Variations:
- Whole-Class Same First Line: In quick succession, have partners play one scene either with or against. The next set of partners plays the scene with the same initiation as the first group but a different response. Continue having the class use the same first line for all scenes, seeing how many different possible with and against responses there are.

Behavior/Context

A clearly defined character is a strong character. It does not need to be played with an over-the-top style. Explicitly picking clear characters before you step onstage puts you in a strong place and gives you experience playing from a clear point of view.

Explanation:
Write two series of suggestions on slips of paper. The director may generate them or have the players write them down. The first pile of slips includes either occupations or specific relationships: bank teller, prom date, aunt, doctor, police officer, mother, etc. Each slip in the second pile includes a specific behavior trait, e.g., talks too much, mothering, inept, overly sexual, know-it-all, self-loathing, has to be funny, wants to be everyone's best buddy.

(On a following page are examples you can photocopy, cut up, and use.)

Once these piles are created, two players take the stage. One player grabs a slip from each pile, reads them to herself, and starts the scene when ready. Her goal is to frustrate her partner through application of the behavior on the slip of paper. If she has a very specific occupation or relationship, she needs to be overt with her initiation to convey it to her partner. The other actor, who did not get slips of paper, is to play the scene as the straight man, the more real character, and to be frustrated by the behaviors of the initiator. After the scene, if you wish, the actor who played straight man can try and guess what was on the paper slips, but that part is completely for fun. Success or failure in this exercise should be measured by the power of the scene that happened onstage, not by an actor's ability to get her partner to guess what's on arbitrary paper slips.

Coaching Points:
- Initiators may worry about playing their suggestion "right." This is not a guessing game. Your suggestion is not projected on a screen for the audience to see and judge your performance. Make a clear, definitive choice up top and play the scene.

- Initiators might fail to be clear up top about where the scene is taking place. They must be explicit.

- The responder might add a detail that undermines the suggestion. Tell him to "yes" without "anding" until he understands the scene the initiator wants to play. This could take five lines.

- The responder – the straight man – must experience an emotional rise, based not on the circumstance but on the behavior of the initiator. When he's pinched, he must say ouch.

- Initiators might fixate on playing their choice and not really live in the moment. They must be willing to relent, apologize, or admit their fault to keep the scene going.

-Responders are allowed to threaten to leave, cancel the date, or do whatever is appropriate to keep the situation believable. It's not their job to stay in the scene through artificial means. As per the note above, the initiator must keep her partner onstage, not by physical means but by altering her behavior.

Variations:

- Player's Choice from Inspiration: Using any of the scene game techniques, a monologue or a newspaper article, players are to find their own behaviors and contexts. Perhaps a player tells a truthful monolog to the class and other players take turns starting scenes with inspired behavior context pairs. Ask them afterward what they played, to keep them honest. They should say something simple, two or three words maximum.

Behaviors	Context
bored all the time	cab driver
anal-retentive	waiter
acts like your best buddy	friend
condescending	spouse
mothering	boyfriend / girlfriend
gullible	flight attendant
lazy repair	person
has to be funny	parent
cries easily	police officer
no sense of humor	bartender
self-conscious	co-worker
incompetent	boss
sexy	ice cream salesperson
nauseatingly sunny	professor
creepy	classmate
arrogant	doctor
"Gothic" dark	date
finishes others thoughts	therapist

General Agreement Scenes

While not every scene requires matching characters, the ability to do it illustrates an actor's ability to listen, observe, and create in the moment.

Explanation:
Two players take the stage with a designated initiator. The initiator makes a character choice and begins the scene with a line indicative of that character. The responder matches the character. Physicality and vocal matching are less important than point-of-view matching.

Coaching Points:
- The initiator must make a clear choice. Archetypes are a good place to start.

- The responder must not play against. He must also not play "with" in words but "against" in attitude.

- The initiation must not put the responder automatically in an against position.

- Once the scene has started, encourage the players to radically change the subject of their conversation.

- Encourage matching points of view with different characters. For example, the captain of the cheerleaders and the quarterback of the football team are different characters who share a similar point of view.

Variations:
- Group Scenes: What makes group scenes (three or more actors) confusing isn't the number of actors but the number of points of view. With three actors

onstage, ask two to play with (to match characters) and one to play against. A teenager coming home to a concerned mom and dad would be a good example. Try this with four, five, and more actors, always limiting the points of view to two.

- Click, Click, Boom: Two actors onstage. One is designated "it." The actors start the scene in general agreement. After five or six exchanges, and when "it" feels comfortable, "it" must introduce an absurdity to shift the scene from with to against. "Not it" must not accommodate the absurdity, but be negatively affected by it. Perhaps, after ten lines of a low-key fixing-dinner scene, "it" decides to spit in the chili because that's what Grandma always did. "Not it" is disgusted.

Machine Characters

By creating a character's physicality first, we highlight emotion, active choices, and unpredictability over witty dialogue.

Explanation:
Three actors onstage: A, B, and C. Actor A begins a machine as one might in a Machine Building exercise (see instructions below if you are new to machine building). Actor B joins the machine in a complementary fashion. After actor B has found her machine rhythm, actor A is excused from the stage. Actor C takes the stage, assuming a neutral posture. Actor B will transform her machine posture, motion, and noise into a character voice and movement. She will also initiate the scene verbally in a fashion appropriate to her physicality. Actor C is to respond to the behavior and words.

Whole-Class Machine Building in brief:
A player takes the stage and begins making a short, repetitive motion with her body. She also makes a repetitive noise to go along with the motion. A player joins the player onstage creating a complementary motion and noise. The idea is that they're both cogs in a machine and they must mesh together, perhaps even touch. Players continue to join the growing machine, adding their piece to any existing piece, always making sure to connect with what's already onstage.

Coaching Points
- The machine physicality IS NOT an activity that the player was just performing. It is an emotional gesture that exists only to help actor B find an outside-in character.

- Keep machines and resultant characters varied and committed. Ask actors, especially those starting machines, to take risks with their bodies and voices. Machines may also be slow and purposeful, especially if, after several people have had their turn, all of the resulting characters have been frantic.

- The responding player (C) has to give some latitude to the gestures of the machine-born character. He can't just stand back and call out the weird motions.

Variations:
- Two Machine Characters: A fourth player, D, is added to provide a physical inspiration for actor C. Then B and C play a scene, each with an outside-in character.